URZILA CARLSON

Rolling with the Punchlines

a memoir

URZILA CARLSON

Rolling with the Punchlines

a memoir

This edition published in 2020
First published in 2016

Allen & Unwin
83 Alexander Street
Crows Nest NSW 2065
Australia
Phone: (61 2) 8425 0100
Email: info@allenandunwin.com
Web: www.allenandunwin.com

EU Authorised Representative: Easy Access System Europe, Mustamäe tee 50, 10621 Tallinn, Estonia, gpsr.requests@easproject.com

A catalogue record for this book is available from the National Library of Australia

ISBN 978 1 98854 772 5

Set in Plantin
Printed in Australia by Pegasus Media & Logistics

10 9 8 7 6 5 4

The paper in this book is FSC® certified. FSC® promotes environmentally responsible, socially beneficial and economically viable management of the world's forests.

To my family, the ones that live in the house with me, the ones who live abroad, the friends I've had for years or the friends I've made recently: you are all part of my life and part of who I am, who I will one day be and I am part of you. Thank you, thank you for sharing my life with me and for letting me share yours. I'm thankful that I discovered early on that it's not things or money, it's people that matter, and I'm fortunate to have some of the best people in my life. Thankfully I have very powerful people who surround me, people who understand that at the end of the day, it's not who climbs the ladder fastest; people who know that after all of the shit has hit the fan, we still need to stand up, hold up and support each other and carry on for our kids and our loves; people who give you the nod and say: 'Don't worry. We've got this!' I'm thankful to the people in my life who make sure my heart stays open and receptive, and I understand that when you're lucky, you meet the people you love early in life and walk with them a long road. Others we meet later and have to keep them close in the time we have but, either way, we must acknowledge that life is short and we have to make it count while we are here. I love you all!* My life may not be perfect but it is near perfect.

*Well, obviously not ALL of you. But I'm quite fond of most of you.

CONTENTS

PROLOGUE ____ 9
THE ONE ABOUT THE BIG BABY ____ 12
THE ONE ABOUT HAPPY FAMILIES ____ 24
THE ONE ABOUT POOR BUT HAPPY ____ 35
THE ONE ABOUT SCHOOL BEING THE HAPPIEST DAYS OF MY LIFE ____ 44
THE ONE ABOUT MY SHIP COMING IN ____ 58
THE ONE ABOUT MY NORMAL KIDNEY ____ 67
THE WHOLE APARTHEID ROUTINE ____ 74
THE ONE ABOUT OUT OF AFRICA ____ 82
THE ONE ABOUT ME TAKING ORDERS ____ 93
SIX SOUTH AFRICANS, ONE SPANIARD AND THE WELSH . . . ____ 104
THE ONE ABOUT SETTLING RIGHT BACK IN ____ 113
THERE'S THIS GIRL IN A CLOSET, RIGHT . . . ____ 118
THE ONE ABOUT OUT OF AFRICA ALL OVER AGAIN ____ 126
THE ONE ABOUT THE LAND OF MILK AND HONEY ____ 139
THE ONE ABOUT THE BREAK-UP ____ 150

THE ONE ABOUT ODD JOBS 155
THE ONE ABOUT A STAR IS BORN 162
TAKE MY WIFE – PLEASE! 171
THE ONE ABOUT STARTING OUT IN COMEDY 175
THE ONE ABOUT WAXING LYRICAL 182
THE ONE ABOUT THE MOUSE 187
THE ONE ABOUT DOING ANAL 192
THE ONE ABOUT THE LITTLE SCREEN 198
THE ONE ABOUT ANTI-SOCIAL MEDIA 204
THE ONE ABOUT AN AUCKLAND SCHOOLTEACHER ENDING APARTHEID 221
THE ONE ABOUT THE BAG LADY 225
THE ONE ABOUT CRACKING AUSTRALIA 232
THERE'S THESE TWO LESBIANS WHO WANT TO HAVE A BABY . . . 237
THE ONE ABOUT THE JOY OF CHILDBIRTH 245
THE ONE ABOUT NOT GETTING MARRIED 249
THE ONE ABOUT THE CAKE 258
THE UNFUNNY ONE ABOUT NUMBER TWO 262
THE ONE ABOUT MAKING IT (SO FAR) 269
EPILOGUE 280

PROLOGUE

If you're reading this, it's probably because you live down under and you've been to my shows or seen me on TV. I've been popping up on telly in New Zealand for a while, but of late I've been trying to give it a crack in Australia, too. And it seems I've found my rhythm with the Aussies . . . a bit like a kangaroo that hops along beside the freeway at speed, just managing to stay off the tarmac and stay alive!

I'm not even sure when Australia started taking over my time. It's almost like a drinking problem. Everyone else noticed first and they were all talking about it, but I had no idea. After all, it's not that long ago that I did my first performance in Australia. I could have counted the number of people in the audience on one hand. In fact, that's actually what I did. In the terms we were discussing, it was the equivalent of a small shandy. But now it's almost got out of hand. I spend half a year in the Lucky Country, to the point where I gather that in New Zealand comedy circles, there has long been speculation about my status and whether or not I'll move to Australia for good. I find it fascinating that location matters to other comics. Most people in my audiences don't even know where I live. When I'm in Melbourne, they assume I'm Sydney-based and vice versa. They'd all probably be surprised to learn that I'm actually based in West Auckland in New Zealand.

> **"I'M NOT EVEN SURE WHEN AUSTRALIA STARTED TAKING OVER MY TIME. IT'S ALMOST LIKE A DRINKING PROBLEM. EVERYONE ELSE NOTICED FIRST."**

All the same, the speculation seems to have spread to my family. I've lived in South Africa, America, Wales and New Zealand, and it seems my mother is to this day not keen on me moving to Australia. A while back, she and my sister moved to Christchurch in New Zealand's South Island. My mom said to me one weekend she was visiting that she would cut me — we're a very expressive family — if I moved again. I've tried to point out that it's really not that much harder to visit Sydney or Melbourne from Christchurch than it is to visit Auckland, and that the person who will be most affected if I shift across the ditch will be my brother. But funnily enough, I don't see that much of him either, perhaps because he lives so close anyway. We don't have dinners at each other's houses, we don't spend weekends around a BBQ and talk shit about the week. I ring him if I need him and he does the same. Occasionally we will go for a drive or attempt to go fishing, but realistically, we probably live too close to each other to hang out. When you live super close to someone you tend to take them for granted: you don't make time to visit — why would you? They live four blocks away, for crying out loud! It's when they live far away that you put them in the diary, you book tickets and hire a car, you have time off work, you put the EFFORT in and actually visit . . . What I'm saying is, it probably won't be a hundred years before I move to Australia. It just makes sense. I spend half of my professional life there. Mom will understand — or the crazy African mama will cut me, who knows.

If you'd told me when I was a child in South Africa, or even when I first started out in comedy, that I'd be having this conversation with myself as I sat contemplating my keyboard, trying not to lose it at my children or the dog or my wife for making TOO MUCH FUCKING NOISE FOR A BODY TO GET ANY WORK DONE, I'd have laughed. I'm a comic, you see, and I know a good joke when I see one. But if I've learned one thing in life, it's that truth can be not only stranger than fiction, but also more ironic. And here I am, Exhibit A, literally sitting in Auckland but figuratively big in Australia and with international festival appearances and even a Netflix credit to my name, smiling at the irony of it all (on the inside, because at the same time I have to scowl at my wife, dog and kids if I'm to get any peace and quiet).

It's been quite a ride, from my unpromising beginnings to the glittering heights I now occupy, with (just saying) a NETFLIX CREDIT to my name. Join me as I look back. Or just skip to the final chapter, where I mention, among other things, MY NETFLIX SPECIAL.

The One About THE BIG BABY

I was born in South Africa in 1976. I think for most South Africans, my birth was probably overshadowed by events in Soweto, and, even in my most egotistical moments, I'll admit this is probably fair enough. We'll talk more about Soweto later. In the meantime, back to me!

It was raining in Johannesburg on 15 February 1976, or so I'm told. The rain is part of the legend. Another part is that I was — and remain to this day — the biggest baby ever to have been born in the Queen Victoria Hospital. That's what the nuns told Mom, and nuns aren't allowed to lie. Lettie (my mother) reckons she was in labour with me for more than a week. Mom isn't a nun, so she has been known to lie, or at least gild the lily a bit. But it's safe to believe her when she says it was an epic labour and that at some point the nuns

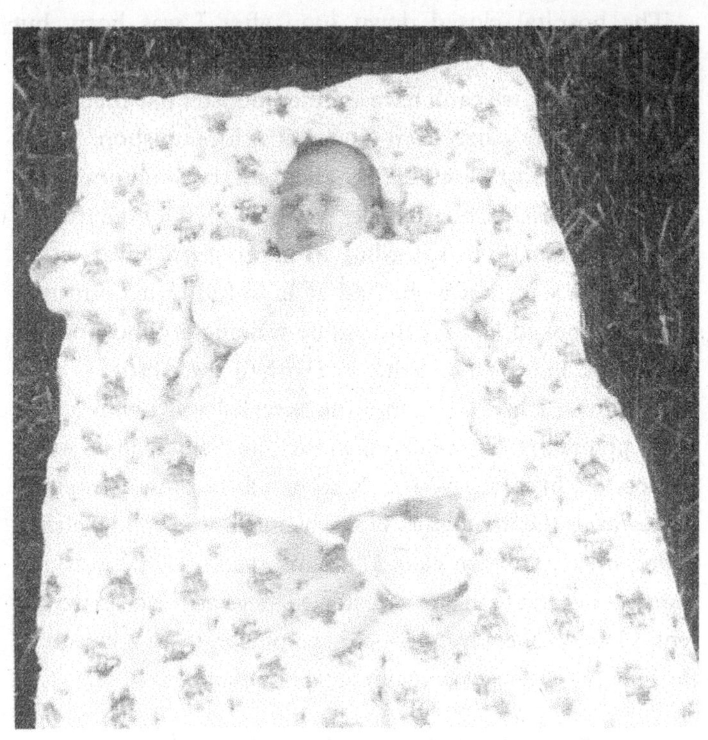

This is me at four weeks old. Just look at that pout!

feared she would lose her life, or I would lose mine, or both. I can't remember much about it, but to this day I'm not fond of confined spaces, so it must have left an impression on me, too.

The hospital closed down soon after I was born, but that was probably just a coincidence. I don't think the nuns thought, 'Fuck, we can't have another monster like that again, ever. It's clearly a sign from God. Let's close up shop.'

Delivering an 11-pound (5.5-kilogram) baby naturally will always be stressful, but actually Mom dodged a bullet. I was a month premature. According to my mother, I was so big the doctors said that if she had gone to full term with me I would've looked like a baby giraffe walking around on little hippo legs. I used to love that story when I was little.

As it was, I had to go into the neonatal ward with all the other premature babies. Most premature babies don't weigh 11 pounds. In fact, if you scooped up all the other premature babies from the incubators in the neonatal ward and weighed them, they probably wouldn't have made 11 pounds put together. I didn't fit in an incubator, so they had me in an oxygen tent. I looked like a five-year-old camping in there amongst all the little plastic boxes containing tiny human beings.

I am the youngest of three, with an older brother, Quintin, and an older sister, Reinette. I once asked my mother if she knew I was going to be the youngest child. Her response was, 'No, but I hoped so.' That always stuck with me.

I brought it up with my brother once when I was about 11. He looked me right in the eye and said, 'I'll tell you what happened. First Mom had me and she looked at me and she thought, "What an adorable baby. Let's have another one." Then she had our sister and looked at her and said, "Oh my god! What a beautiful, beautiful baby! Let's have another one!" Then she had you, looked at you and said "Ewwww! We are DONE!"'

My brother is really quite a sensitive soul and probably didn't mean to scar me for life. And he didn't. The saving grace of my family is that we can all take a joke. And the other saving grace is that we can all give as good as we get.

I smiled at him.

> **"THE SAVING GRACE OF MY FAMILY IS THAT WE CAN ALL TAKE A JOKE. AND THE OTHER SAVING GRACE IS THAT WE CAN ALL GIVE AS GOOD AS WE GET."**

'You're an asshole,' I said sweetly.

Even at the tender age of 11, I knew a bit about how babies are made, and that it is basically the same thing as making pancakes (although even at the tender age of 11 I had an inkling that the ingredients were a bit different).

'What happened,' I told Quintin and Reinette, 'was the same thing that happens when you make pancakes. The first two are usually flops. There are so many things that can go wrong, and do go wrong, when you make pancakes or babies that you look at the first couple and you're happy you made them, but they just aren't right. It's only the third pancake that's the perfect pancake. Basically what I'm saying is I am the perfect pancake. I am the perfect child. Mom knew that she didn't need to tweak the recipe, because she's got the perfect one. Also, just like with pancakes, you don't throw the first few munters out. You keep them, you eat them. You just don't cherish them like the perfect one.'

'Fair enough,' laughed Quintin.

The perceptive amongst you will have noticed we talked about Mom making pancakes and babies as though she was doing it all on her own. Well, she basically was. Mom was actually living in Natal while she was pregnant with me, but as she was approaching the big day (and obviously I use the term 'big' advisedly) she and Dad went with Reinette and Quintin to visit my grandmother in Johannesburg. Dad sauntered off one day to get some bread and milk and didn't come back till I was six months old. The first time I met him, my mother put six-month-old me on his chest and I apparently gave him one look, wound my little fingers into his luxuriant chest hair and ripped out a good couple of handfuls. That didn't help the already much-impaired bonding process. In fact, we never got on. He often said I'm not his and I've often hoped I wasn't.

Once Dad came back — in body at least, if not in spirit — we returned to our home in Hlobane, a little town in Natal where my father worked as a miner and my mother as a bookkeeper at the train station. It should have been quite an idyllic childhood: we got to drive locomotives up and down the railway yards and stuff like that, thanks to Mom, and what kid wouldn't kill to get some of that action? All the good bits

The three of us having an ice block. Note there's not one smile. I'm the one keeping a *very* close eye on mine.

The three of us in double denim. Note, Reinette and I are dressed the same. I'm crying here — it's almost as if I knew I wouldn't cry as an adult so I had to get it all out as a child.

were thanks to Mom. All the bad bits were down to Dad, his alcoholism and his abuse. In the end, it all got too much, and when I was eight, my parents got divorced.

At least, that's the quick and easy way to describe what happened. What really happened is that one night we climbed into our neighbour's car and lay flat on the floor as he drove us out of town to safety, with Dad all the while rampaging around with a handgun, looking for us. Our neighbour drove us to the home of friends of his in a nearby town, Vryheid. They hid us for the night. While I didn't have a clear idea of what was going on, I do remember that in their house I felt completely safe for the first time in my life. I've never met them or heard of them since, but along with the neighbour who bravely drove us away that night, I have no doubt they saved our lives. If it hadn't been for them, neither I, my siblings nor my mother would be here today.

In the morning, my uncle collected us and drove us to Germiston on the East Rand of Johannesburg. It was only four and a half hours, but it felt like a full day in the car. At the end of the journey, I was back in the house where I had spent the first six months of my life. Funny, but it didn't ring any bells at all.

Ouma Lettie, my grandmother (my mom was named after her), lived there with Oom Boet, my uncle. It wasn't a huge house, and all four of us — my mom, both my siblings and I — lived in one bedroom. My grandmother was wheelchair-bound because of a stroke, but she didn't take an ounce of shit, ever. She'd sit in her chair in the doorway of her room with a strategic view of the other rooms and the lounge. If you said something to annoy her, she'd reach behind her to where her slipper bag was hanging behind the door. She wore slippers all the time — the type with the hard plastic soles — but she also kept a few spares to use as ammunition whenever we stepped out of line. That woman had an amazing arm. Whenever she reached behind that door, we started running, but she'd always get you in the back or on the back of the head. There was no escape. My grandmother was very religious, so it was quite easy to offend her. Even saying you were bored was enough. After the slipper strike, she'd put you to work, and would work you to bits, presumably to save you from what happens to those with idle hands.

When you're eight years old, the world is full of temptations, and that's probably why I sustained so many head injuries from flying slippers as a child. One of the biggest temptations was right across the road from the house. None of us kids had ever seen a mine dump before, but it was love at first sight. It was about the size of a mountain, but it was made of what felt like beach sand. You could climb it if you got a good run-up, and coming down in giant strides — often falling flat on your face and tumbling over and over in the fine dirt — was a total blast.

"WHEN YOU'RE EIGHT YEARS OLD, THE WORLD IS FULL OF TEMPTATIONS."

My mom and my grandmother used to lecture us at length on the dangers of the mine dump, and we took these warnings to heart. I clearly remember one day Quintin and I discussed the dangers, and decided we needed to protect ourselves. So we went into my uncle's sock drawer. There was a .38-calibre pistol in one sock, a little .22 in another and a sock full of ammunition, so we loaded the guns, stuffed them in our pants and headed up the dump. What could possibly go wrong? Once high up and out of everyone's view, we lined up some soft-drink cans and bottles and started blazing away at them. The .38 was a bit of a shock: neither of us expected it to kick back so hard or to make our ears ring in quite the way it did. My brother stood behind me, bracing me with his body and covering my ears as I took my turn shooting at the cans.

One of the things they teach you about safety with firearms — apart from the need to keep them in a secure place, such as a sock drawer — was that you shouldn't fire at a target on the skyline. The bullet can keep going for quite a long way, you see, and endanger anything that happens to be on the other side. It so happened that there was an off-duty police officer on his bicycle on the other side while I was firing at the cans. He and a mate were minding their own business when a softnose .38 slug slammed into the frame of his bike close to the pedals. He must have been quite brave, because he immediately set off up the mine dump to find the person who had just shot his bike. He found two very surprised and relatively heavily armed little kids, and started yelling at us.

We heard the bit about him being an off-duty cop, but we didn't wait around to find out if it was true or if he had a badge. We legged it. We weren't pushing bikes and, because we had been up the dump so much, we knew where to run to avoid the sink holes and sand traps. We got down in no time and well ahead of him and his mate, and we hid on top of the roof of my uncle's shed till my mother got home. Then we snuck the guns back into the sock drawer. For years, people were talking about the kids who shot an off-duty officer's bicycle frame and how it nearly killed him. I never corrected

The three of us at our grandparents' house.
No smiles. Just three scared kids.

them and told them it probably would have just gone through his calf, but, you know, it scared the bejesus out of me. I realised that all it could take was a stupid decision and the shit that you can fit into a sock to fuck up your entire life.

Nobody got hurt, but, in my grandmother's words, it was 'only by the grace of God!' that I didn't touch a gun again for years, and when I did I was an adult, it was my brother's gun and he had a licence and sock drawer of his own. Actually, I think he had a gun safe. I do remember we used paper targets set up against a solid wall, and he didn't need to brace me against the recoil any more, as by then I had what you might call a well-developed centre of gravity.

We were living in a pretty small community, and a religious one at that, so there was naturally quite a lot of curiosity — everyone was nosey as fuck, actually — about why my parents had got divorced. The other kids used to tease me about it, because none of their parents were divorced. Even my teachers would ask me why my parents got a divorce. I was eight years old — I had no idea what to say to them. I told Mom that the teachers wanted to know and she told me exactly what to say. So the next time I was asked, I said: 'Miss, it's my dad's fault. My mom realllllyyy, reallllly wanted to be a widow but my dad wouldn't drink the poison.'

To my surprise, the teacher laughed her head off. Mom had written my first ever joke, and I had delivered it with feeling, even if I had no real idea why it was funny. Despite my faint confusion, I knew I had nailed it. I couldn't wait for someone else to ask me why my parents had got divorced.

Ouma Lettie (pre-stroke) standing out in front of the house we fled to.

The One About HAPPY FAMILIES

So far, apart from my deadshit dad, everything sounds kinda wholesome and functional, doesn't it? I mean, like most people in the Western world, I grew up in a nuclear family. It's just that my experience of the nuclear family is much more like the experience of a neutron in the last moments of an atom bomb. Bear with me as I walk you through my family history. You'll see what I mean.

My family is as Afrikaner as you can get. My forefathers marched over the Drakensberg, and we eat dried meat, dabble in casual racism, fear the Lord and attend church on Sundays. Maybe it's all the trekking they did, or the salt in the biltong, or all that lusty singing in church, but, like most Afrikaner families, mine is congenitally very thirsty. In fact, whenever a member of my family settles in a given locale,

Me and Reinette, kitted out the same again. We were entering that phase where the two of us looked like before-and-after photos . . . I started to resemble a horrible warning dressed as my sister.

a number of shebeens — sly grog shops — soon spring up around them. Some of these shebeens will find that they can't keep up, because it's quite common for my family to stock up with drink for the weekend on Friday, then find we're completely out of the stuff on Saturday morning. Saturday morning's shopping trip will keep us going until the evening. Saturday evening is usually spent touring the shebeens in search of one we haven't yet drunk dry, to try to set ourselves up for the Lord's day, the long, dry Sunday to come.

When I say 'we', I don't really include myself in this number. And it wouldn't be fair to include my mom. I can count on one hand the number of drinks she's had during my lifetime and I've never seen her even tipsy.

On the other side of the ledger, I should also point out that we have eight ministers of the Lord on my mother's side. One of them, Oom Herman, is one of my favourite uncles. In 1987, I was riding my bicycle on a gravel road when I hit a deep patch and skidded over. The handlebar narrowly missed taking my eye out, and instead fractured my cheekbone. I was left with a chip out of the bone and if you see me smile you'll notice the right cheek has a bigger ball than the left one. I was off school for a long time, and Oom Herman looked after me. I would lie in the lounge while he worked away, preparing sermons. He made me laugh so much, which hurt like hell in the early days of the injury. He told me one of the funniest stories I've ever heard in my life. He did missionary work throughout Africa and India and one day he dropped into the home of a deacon in his church who had strayed a bit. Before they settled down to read the Bible and pray together, the deacon's wife asked if he'd like a cup of tea.

'Yes, please,' Oom Herman replied. 'I'd love a cup of tea. Milk and two sugars, if you don't mind.'

She went into the kitchen, and Oom Herman heard her busily filling the kettle and clattering cups. Then she swore.

'Which one of you left the sugar open?' she snapped at her children. 'The cat pissed in it again!'

There was a pause. Then in she came, smiling sweetly and carrying his cup of tea. That was awkward, but luckily she went back into the kitchen to fetch some biscuits. Oom Herman took the opportunity to quickly empty his cup into the pot plant on the table beside him. She walked back in with the biscuits and sat down opposite him. There was a trickling noise beside him. He turned his head and they both watched in silence as the tea slowly drained from the fake plant onto the tiles. Oom Herman nibbled his undunked gingernut. Shortly afterwards, he left. He never went back, and that family never appeared in church again. Now that's a peaceful resolution, if ever I've heard of one!

> **"HE WAS A VERY RELIGIOUS MAN BUT HE WASN'T JUDGEMENTAL. HE ACCEPTED US AS WE WERE, AND TREATED US VERY WELL."**

Whenever I think of Oom Herman I think of that story and it puts a smile on my face. He was a very religious man but he wasn't judgemental. He accepted us as we were, and treated us very well. His wife, on the other hand, was my mother's foster sister and she never liked us much and wasn't very nice to us. He recently passed away from cancer. When I heard the news, I hoped that wherever he wound up he is seated near to a pot plant with solid absorption capacity, a homemade gingernut on his plate and no cats for miles.

My grandmother was a very religious woman, too. As

far as she was concerned, the means justified the ends. All kinds of things were OK if they saved souls: violence, lies . . . especially lies.

She used to sit there and say things like: 'Your tannie [aunty] killed your grandfather in the lounge.' That one got our attention. According to her version of events, Tannie Betty had told her father that she had given her four babies away, and the shock was so great that he keeled over from a heart attack. 'Always remember,' my grandmother would say, leaning in close and holding up a righteous finger, 'that bad news can kill your mother. Love Jesus and she will be all right.'

> **"ALL KINDS OF THINGS WERE OK IF THEY SAVED SOULS: VIOLENCE, LIES . . . ESPECIALLY LIES."**

That scared me more than a sock drawer full of guns. How, I wondered, would I know whether the news I was bearing was bad enough to be life-threatening? And, while I dimly perceived that my grandmother was thinking along the lines of teenage pregnancy, I wasn't altogether sure I knew how loving Jesus was meant to prevent stuff like that. I was only eight, after all.

It turns out that my Tannie Betty had her four children adopted out because she couldn't cope. In more recent years, she has been diagnosed as bipolar, which is a slightly better explanation than the accepted family one that 'she is a shit mother'. Nor did she, in fact, kill my grandfather. The culprit was actually their biological son, my uncle — the one with the guns in the sock drawer. He apparently fell asleep at the wheel of their Opel Rekord while they were on their way to Durban for a holiday. The vehicle left the road and flipped over, whereupon his dad (my grandfather) was ejected through the windscreen and the car rolled over him a few times. That's what killed him, but 'always wear a seatbelt, kids' lacked the necessary religious instructive value for my grandmother's tastes. Oh well. She meant well and she loved Jesus so much she had a church built onto her home in the sixties; services were held there three days a week. This definitely helped to cure me of my curiosity about church. I learned more about religious people than I did the finer points of doctrine, but it was also a good experience living there.

Now when I say 'my grandmother' that's not quite accurate. I *knew* her as my grandmother, but she wasn't really my grandmother. She was the woman who raised my mother after my mom and her brother and sister were put in care by the state because my mother's biological parents couldn't look after them. My biological grandparents had another child who wasn't immunised — vaccinate your kids, assholes — and became sick and died. That sent my biological grandparents off the edge. My grandfather (my real grandfather) started drinking a lot, and one day when he was pissed and driving a schoolbus, he ran over and killed a child. To make matters worse — in case they needed making worse — the accident happened right in front of the kid's friends, brothers and cousins. We know this because years later my mother dated one of the cousins. She never told him that it was her father who had killed his cousin. My grandfather went to prison for seven years, and never amounted to much after that, either. I knew him well enough not to like him very much. He remarried later in life, and died of a diabetes-related disease.

My grandmother — my real grandmother, my mother's

biological mother — had gone through trauma long before her daughter died and her husband killed a child and went to jail. When she was a kid, she was sitting in a car outside a hospital in Rhodesia (now Zimbabwe), waiting for her father (my great-grandfather). He was in the hospital visiting his wife (her mother), who was very sick after giving birth to the couple's third child. My grandmother was holding the newborn baby, a little boy, and her sister was in the car, too. They were sitting there waiting when a couple tapped on the window and told my grandmother that her parents had asked them to come and get the baby. My grandmother, who was only nine, handed the boy over. That was the last his family saw of him for 20 years. My biological great-grandmother passed away soon afterwards, never knowing that her baby was gone. The police soon gave up looking, but my great-grandfather — the one who died in the car accident — never gave up the search for the boy. He ran ads in the paper every year for years.

The family eventually moved to South Africa. My great-grandfather remarried, to the champion slipper-throwing woman in the wheelchair who I knew as my grandmother. When the missing boy turned 21, the couple who had kidnapped him outside the hospital that day in Rhodesia showed him the adverts and articles about him, which they had been collecting for years. He looked my great-grandfather up, and it turned out they lived only a few blocks away from one another — weird, but probably no weirder than everything else about this story. My great-grandfather never reported the couple and they were never prosecuted. The boy (or young man, as he had become) kept in touch, but his relationship with his kidnappers never changed. As far as he was concerned, they were his parents.

The person most damaged by the incident was my (real)

grandmother, who grew up to be a very hard woman who drank and had very few fucks to give. She married my (real) grandfather, the bus driver, and they had four children: Betty, Lettie, Maxie and Gerrie. It was Maxie who died, at the age of seven.

I hope you're following all this. I'd do a wiring diagram, but I'm not sure it would help.

It struck most observers that all four kids looked really different. My wife, who studied genetics, once worked out that, based on the blood type of my biological grandparents, there's no way my mother could be my grandfather's child. Who knows what happened there? But my bipolar aunty Betty — who is five years older than my mom — told my mother that my grandfather was away a lot and my grandmother had 'friends'.

Now, when Maxie, my mother's sister, died (from a preventable disease, diphtheria: see the earlier lesson on immunisation) and the state took Mom — who was two — and her two siblings off my grandparents, my grandmother said they should be put up for adoption. But my great-grandfather, who had lost his son and his wife all those years back, convinced his wheelchair-bound Christian wife to foster his three grandchildren, and she agreed. She also fostered other children at times. I understand it's pretty common for foster kids to have issues. My mother often feels like she doesn't belong, even though she always knew her biological parents (assuming the man she assumed was her dad *was* her dad). In fact, we had a good relationship with her mother (my real grandmother) in later years. We'd go visit her in the school holidays. She was, as previously mentioned, hard as old biltong, but very smart and good fun to hang out with. I loved her a lot.

**Running on my mom's friends' farm — smiling, free.
We visited this farm fairly regularly.**

You come to this stage of the story and you wonder what the point of it all was. Well, spare a thought for me. I'm writing it, and even I can't remember what the point of it is.

Wait a minute. Yes, that was it. I think I meant it all to be a defence of my grandmother (not my real one; the other one, my step-great-grandmother with the throwing arm and the slippers). She wasn't our blood, she worked us to bits, she brutalised us with comfy footwear and she never lost a chance to try to save our souls, even if she had to invent a pretext. But she raised my mom, and she took us in when my deadshit dad ran away and then again when we ran away from my deadshit dad, and in the 18 months we lived with her the second time around, my mother was able to save enough to buy a house of our own.

"BY THE TIME I WAS NINE, I COULD COOK A ROAST MEAL FOR A FAMILY OF SIX BY MYSELF, EVEN MAKING DECENT GRAVY TO GO WITH IT."

Because she couldn't move very easily, my grandmother taught me how to cook.

'Get the medium pot out,' she'd say. 'Put a cup of rice in it and fill it with water until it reaches the first knuckle on your pointer finger . . .'

By the time I was nine, I could cook a roast meal for a family of six by myself, even making decent gravy to go with it. Plus I got her family name instead of Bianca, which is what I would have got if we'd been living with my deadshit dad in Durban just after I was born. My mother felt she owed it to her foster-mother to hand on the family names. I love my names.

So what I'm trying to say is that, while my grandmother was strict, she's all good by me. I loved her to bits, and I'm grateful for everything she did for us.

And as for my mom, who has always wondered who she belonged to, well, that's simple. She belongs to us!

The One About POOR BUT HAPPY

In 1985, soon after I turned nine, my mother was given a very second-hand lounge suite. Most families wouldn't consider this to be a red-letter day, but we did. When she wasn't at work Mom got busy re-covering the suite, and, when it was ready, we moved out of my grandmother's house at last. The same uncle who had brought us to safety 18 months before drove us and our lovely new-to-us lounge suite to our very own house in Benoni, a mining town about 30 minutes' drive from Johannesburg in the East Rand. At first glance, it doesn't look like the most promising place to make a new start in life. The town's name is a Hebrew word meaning 'Son of My Sorrow', and the town itself is surrounded by a halo of dumps from goldmines that have nothing left to offer. Put it this way: if you had two captains choosing towns to be on their team, you'd have to think Benoni would be the one left over at the end.

The first thing we noticed as we drove in were the towering mine dumps. My brother and I looked at them approvingly.

'You're not allowed to play on those,' my mother said sternly.

Once in town, we drove past a series of lakes. As we drove past the middle lake — called, well, Middle Lake — my brother and I looked out eagerly over the sparkling water surrounded by willow trees.

'I don't want you kids swimming in there,' said my mother.

It seems, looking back, that I spent my entire childhood swimming and fishing in Middle Lake, but that can't be right, because a lot of the time, my brother and I would also ride our bikes out to the mine dumps on the edge of town and play there all day, imagining we were at the beach, or constructing jumps for our bikes. Quite apart from the dangers of the unstable heaps themselves, Mom told us there would be all kinds of undesirable people hanging out there, smoking pot and God knows what else, but we weren't interested in that. We just wanted to hang out. I swam and fished and biked and ran and jumped in all the open spaces that Benoni offered until my chest burned.

There was also the Benoni Bunny Park. I used to think of the Bunny Park and wonder if there was any other town in the world with such visionary city fathers. Looking back, I realise that they were just making a virtue of necessity — they had fenced off all the rabbits that infested a particular open space in the middle of town in an effort to try to contain them, and an ice-cream van had opportunistically set up there — to me, it was like Disneyland, only with more and better rabbits. I wasn't alone in thinking this. My primary school often took us there for a day out, and it was still a major attraction until very recently, when it was deemed too run-down and was closed. I was sad to read that. I don't know what they did with the bunnies.

Another of Benoni's unique attractions was Tom Jones Street. Legend has it that the Welsh crooner once came to visit Benoni and the town loved him so much it changed the name of the main street to honour him. It was a cruel blow to learn this was not the case. It turns out the street was named after a town councillor. I don't even think he could sing, and if anyone ever chucked their panties at him, history hasn't recorded it.

> **"IT'S A WEIRD FEELING GOOGLING YOUR HOME TOWN. IT'S A BIT LIKE GOOGLING YOUR MOM — IT FEELS LIKE YOU'RE INVADING HER PRIVACY, BUT YOU KNOW YOU'LL FIND STUFF THAT WILL MAKE YOU PROUD."**

You might think I'm trying too hard now, but I recently learned that the former Olympic swimmer Charlene Wittstock, these days the Princess Consort of Monaco, was born in Benoni. I decided I would google my home town to see who else it would turn up. It's a weird feeling googling your home town. It's a bit like googling your mom — it feels like you're invading her privacy, but you know you'll find stuff that will make you proud. Turns out Charlize Theron, Oscar-winning actor and all-round good sort, is one of ours. So is Grace, the wife of Zimbabwe's despot Robert Mugabe, so it's not all wins, I suppose.

A mine dump, one of Benoni's most recognisable sights in the eighties and nineties. It has since been levelled and the town now looks like your favourite uncle who is losing his front tooth.

I also learned that the marketing people have been hard at work, so that the place where I grew up is no longer known as Benoni: Son of My Sorrow but as Benoni: City of Lakes. As far as I'm concerned, though, this is one pig that doesn't need any lipstick. I had a wonderful childhood there, and I will never have a bad word to say about Benoni.

*

We grew up dirt poor. Now, I want to clarify 'poor'. Some people have romantic notions of being poor. You often see it in movies, where people will say, 'My father moved to this country with only fifty dollars in his pocket and a dream in his heart.'

"WHEN YOU ARE THAT POOR, YOU ARE ONLY WORRIED ABOUT TOMORROW AND ABOUT SURVIVAL. TAKE IT FROM ME: DREAMS ARE A LUXURY."

Well, we didn't have any money in our pockets and we were too poor to dream. I think only people who have truly been in the situation where they had nothing to their name will understand what I mean when I say there were no dreams. When you are that poor, you are only worried about tomorrow and about survival. Take it from me: dreams are a luxury.

*

Outside Mom's friends' farmhouse as teenagers. I loved my frilly shorts — and, yeah, I wanted to tuck my shirt in.

Apart from the lounge suite, we each had a bed. That's it — no fridge, no electrical appliances, nothing else. All our possessions made for one trailer-load, and would have done to furnish a single room. It made for a pretty empty-looking three-bedroom house. My sister and I shared the big room and my mother and brother each got a small room. We had a polystyrene box that we used to keep our milk cool. Because we didn't have a refrigerator, we couldn't keep lots of groceries chilled, but that was fine, because we couldn't afford lots of groceries. Even when we eventually got a chest freezer, we didn't really stock it up. Town was seven kilometres away and, because we had no car, we had to walk; that was way too far to carry lots of groceries, even if we'd been able to afford them.

We were dirt poor, but we were happy. We had each other, we had the mine dumps and Middle Lake, and, best of all, we also had a mother who was absolutely dedicated to ensuring that we had a happy childhood. We had no TV, but we had a well-used library card. My mother worked 12 hours a day to keep a roof over our heads and food on our plates, but when she was home over weekends, she'd read to us in the garden. We'd always laugh a lot, about everything. We'd tell each other stories and we were always encouraged to use our imagination and to be creative. We'd garden together, and we learned very quickly how to fix things ourselves: my brother and I could fix basically anything.

You'll notice I talk quite a lot about doing stuff with my brother, and not so much about doing stuff with my sister. Reinette was (and is to this day) a big reader. Give her a good book and stand well clear: you won't see her for days. It's not that common for parents to wish that their child would read less, but my mother was always trying to get Reinette to put her book down.

My mom working in the garden at our new house. She loves gardening, which was handy because, as you can see, there was nothing around.

'Put it down and do your homework,' she would say, 'or I'll rip you up and send the book to school.'

Even then, I knew a great line when I heard one.

> **"WE ARE A VERY CLOSE FAMILY AND WE TALK DAILY. I KNOW PEOPLE WHO NEVER TALK TO THEIR FAMILY AND IT MAKES ME SAD FOR THEM."**

Looking back today, I'm glad we had nothing but each other. We are a very close family and we talk daily. I know people who never talk to their family and it makes me sad for them.

Having grown up in poverty has also proved useful.

'We used to go to the zoo a lot as kids,' my wife will say.

'Oh,' I'll reply. 'It must be nice to have grown up with money.'

She was quite slow to catch on at first, but now it's become our little joke.

'Yeah, mate,' she'll say. 'We loved it!'

The One About SCHOOL BEING THE HAPPIEST DAYS OF MY LIFE

Because Reinette and I were so close in age, we were in the same year at school. When we finished primary school, we were both sent off to boarding school in Heidelberg. Quintin also started boarding school at the same time. Heidelberg is only 40 minutes' drive away from Benoni, but some days it felt a lot further. The first time we went there, Uncle Derek drove us and bought our school uniforms for us, because my mom didn't have a car yet and couldn't drive that far even if she did. He picked us up and probably sensed the mood in the car, because he told us jokes all the way to Heidelberg.

He was a very funny man, and we were feeling almost OK about going to boarding school. Our first sight of the place cured us of that. It looked almost military. We were driving around Heidelberg, and I remarked to Uncle Derek that it was pretty intimidating.

'What?' he yelled. 'We are bigger and stronger and way cooler than this school! Come on!'

He drove to the school, straight onto the sports field in front of the main stadium and did a massive burn-out! It was such an immature and stupid thing to do, but it felt great.

"I THINK BOARDING SCHOOL WAS PROBABLY THE BEST THING THAT EVER HAPPENED TO ME. THINK ABOUT IT. IT'S BASICALLY A SLEEPOVER ON A GRAND SCALE."

The burn-out mark was still there five days later when we started school. Everyone was talking about it, the principal was pissed and only the three of us knew who did it. In this day and age, it would have been all over Facebook or Twitter and definitely would have been picked up by CCTV cameras, but back then it was just a crazy uncle making his nieces and nephew feel better about going away to school.

The first month in boarding school was terrible. I missed Mom a lot, and I missed the freedom that I had enjoyed while I was at primary school. But I adjusted quickly, and even though you could never have told me at the time, I think boarding school was probably the best thing that ever happened to me. Think about it. It's basically a sleepover on a grand scale. And if there was ever a place ideally suited to getting you to realise that you prefer girls to boys, boarding school is it. Not that I got up to anything. I was a good girl. Well, even now that I have come out as a lesbyterian — more about that later — I'm a geek rather than a player, and back then I was too shy, and too petrified of burning in hell, which is what the teachers encouraged you to believe was awaiting you if you stepped over that particular line. So nothing ever happened — or nothing more than maybe a pash or two.

So, after the settling-in period, boarding school was fun — so much fun that I didn't really work very hard. I barely passed the first year. I didn't pass the second year. Well, I scraped a technical pass, but Mom decided I should redo the year and try to get better marks. Lettie was a firm believer that you 'shouldn't let a bad year influence the rest of your life'. I was quite angry. Actually, I was really fucking angry. The prospect of redoing a whole school year was humiliating. All my classmates were moving on and here I was, stuck with a bunch of younger kids. Although, actually, they were the same age as me, because of my birthday — I had sort of got ahead of myself in the system. But, funnily enough, no one gave as much of a shit as I did. I wasn't the object of ridicule from my classmates, past or present.

Even when, after about a week, I got over myself and settled into the new school year, though, I wasn't about to let Mom off the hook. Partly this is because she had teamed up with another deadshit man. We'd only been at boarding school a short time when we were told there was a phone call for us. It was Mom, and she told us she was engaged to be married. She had met her new beau through our neighbours — he was a workmate of my Uncle Noel (as we called our neighbour), which seems quite amazing to me now, given the severe aversion he had to work of any description. We'd only met him once before. My first impressions of Mom's new man weren't great, and my opinion only got worse from there as we slowly got to know him.

Still, to give him his due, he did provide us with the first real father figure we'd ever had: his dad, Wes, who was an ex-cop. Wes took us fishing and taught me all sorts of life skills, like paving and tiling and the stuff that lets me hold my own in Kiwi DIY conversations.

“WHEN YOU'RE YOUNG, YOU DON'T NECESSARILY SEE THE LINK BETWEEN HARD WORK AND THINGS GOING RIGHT IN YOUR LIFE.”

My new stepdad was a layabout and a sulker. I didn't want anything to do with him. We didn't get home that much anyway — maybe only once a month — but for three months or so, whenever Mom or my deadshit stepfather showed up to take us home for the weekend, I would hide and flatly refuse to go.

It was around this time that I had a bit of a change of attitude towards school and schoolwork. Neither Quintin nor Reinette could see much value in it and, up to this point, nor could I.

'Poetry!' Reinette used to rage, when directed to do her homework instead of read a book. 'I'm never going to use poetry in my life!'

'Fair enough,' I would think, but by now, I was starting to put in a bit of effort and was therefore reaping the rewards. When you're young, you don't necessarily see the link between hard work and things going right in your life. But I was beginning to see it, dimly. I did much better at my second year the second time around.

Heidelberg Boarding School accepted kids from primary right through to secondary school. Everyone was divided up into halls of residence, and because I was the oldest in my hall (I was 15 by now) I was put in charge of the primary-school kids. There was no status attached to this — I wasn't a prefect or anything — but I had to keep an eye on them. I took this responsibility quite seriously. For this reason, I had a run-in one weekend with a teacher, and that was the beginning of the end of my time at boarding school.

I didn't see eye to eye with that particular teacher, Mr van Heerden. He would send his two kids in to play with the primary-school kids on Sunday mornings so that he could have a sleep-in. Nowadays, that seems fair enough to me — just a parent's natural instinct for any opportunity to sleep in — but back then I sort of resented it.

What made it worse is that if he or his wife got woken up by noisy kids they would punish the kids. Bear in mind that this was South Africa in the late eighties, when corporal punishment of children wasn't just tolerated, it was promoted as the only thing standing between civilisation and chaos. No one — teachers or parents — were too inclined to spare the rod. So, if the little kids were making too much noise being little kids, the wife would come out brandishing a wooden spoon, and it was no idle threat. She would set about the kids with it.

I didn't think that was right. Quite apart from the fact that I thought grown-ups shouldn't hit children with bits of wood, this particular grown-up had no business disciplining the kids at all. So I took the wooden spoon off her in a less-than-polite manner. We had a few words and, of course, I was in trouble. The school called my mother in for a meeting where it was made abundantly obvious that they didn't like me. They couldn't actually expel me just because they didn't like me, and, in any case, I wasn't 16 yet. But they showed Mom a calendar on which they were marking off the days to my sixteenth birthday, and made it clear that they would do their level best to get rid of me as soon as the big day came. My mother did the only decent thing, and took me out of boarding school.

Hoërskool Brandwag (Brandwag High School) was two blocks away from my home in Benoni. I started there on the same day as the new principal. Mr Pieterse called me into his office and said, 'Carlson, I know you've had some trouble with your previous school. But I believe a clean slate means just that: a clean slate. I'm not going to hover the bullshit from the previous school over your head, but I want you to promise not to bring the bullshit from your previous school to this school.'

'Don't call me Carlson,' I muttered under my breath, but I readily agreed to this deal.

Maybe it wasn't just me who he was talking to, but in the first assembly of every term, Mr Pieterse was in the habit of telling the kids, 'If you are here because everything at your old school was horrible — the teachers, the kids, the environment, just everything — and you only have bad things to say, then you will hate it here, too. The problem is you. If you think everyone and everything else is wrong and you are the only one who is right, think again. Don't bad-mouth your old school or friends. Start fresh and keep it positive.'

That's always stuck with me. There's an old saying that wherever you go, there you are. You can change your scenery all you like, but if the problem lives within you there's no way you can escape it. I liked Mr Pieterse and I still do. He was one of the best teachers I ever had, even if it was only this one life lesson he taught me. I never got into trouble at Brandwag. I only had three years of school left and I didn't want to be one of the kids who held on to the shit from my past. Because there was nothing hanging over my head, I didn't feel like I was being watched every second of every day.

> **"THERE'S AN OLD SAYING THAT WHEREVER YOU GO, THERE YOU ARE. YOU CAN CHANGE YOUR SCENERY ALL YOU LIKE BUT IF THE PROBLEM LIVES WITHIN YOU, THERE'S NO WAY YOU CAN ESCAPE IT."**

Another person who changed my life with a few simple words was my homeroom teacher, Mrs Christelle du Plessis. As I was walking out after class one day, she grabbed my arm and held me until it was only me and her left in the classroom. Still holding on, she looked at me and said, 'Carlson, there's no greater waste of time than regret.'

'Don't call me Carlson,' I muttered as I walked out, but it was as though I had heard a penny drop. I kept thinking about what she had said for the rest of that day, for the rest of that week and for the rest of my life. It really made sense. There truly *is* no greater waste of time than regret!

I made this little piece of advice the centre of my TEDx

Talk many years later (we'll come back to that). It doesn't mean you have to try to live the kind of life that gives you no cause for regret. I don't believe that's possible. Nor does it mean you can do and say what you like without giving a fuck. It doesn't mean either of those things. What it means is this: don't waste your time regretting the stuff that has gone wrong. Seize every opportunity life puts in your way, because you only have one life and you have to make the best of it.

When I did my TEDx talk (I can tell you're dying to hear all about it, but I'll come back to it later), I had no idea if it would be watched or if anyone would give a shit about what I had to say, really. To be completely honest with you, I didn't really think about the talk past the day I delivered it. I was asked to do a talk; I did the talk; job done. However, to this day I get feedback from people — either via email, in person or on any form of social media — who say they watched it and it touched a nerve or it meant something to them.

One day, a young man from Australia contacted me and said that he'd watched the 10-minute clip and had been moved to start living his life according to the principle that 'there is no greater waste of time than regret'. So profoundly had the decision changed his life, he said, that he'd had those words tattooed on his side! Now, I'm always a little sceptical when someone says they've had something tattooed on, but I suppose I shouldn't be. Once someone came up to me and said, 'I've got your name tattooed on my butt.' I didn't believe her. But I soon learned that she did have the actual words 'your name' tattooed on her ass! Similarly, the young guy sent me a photo attachment to prove that he really did have Mrs du Plessis's pearl of wisdom inscribed on his flank. I was blown away, but I also thought, 'None of this praise

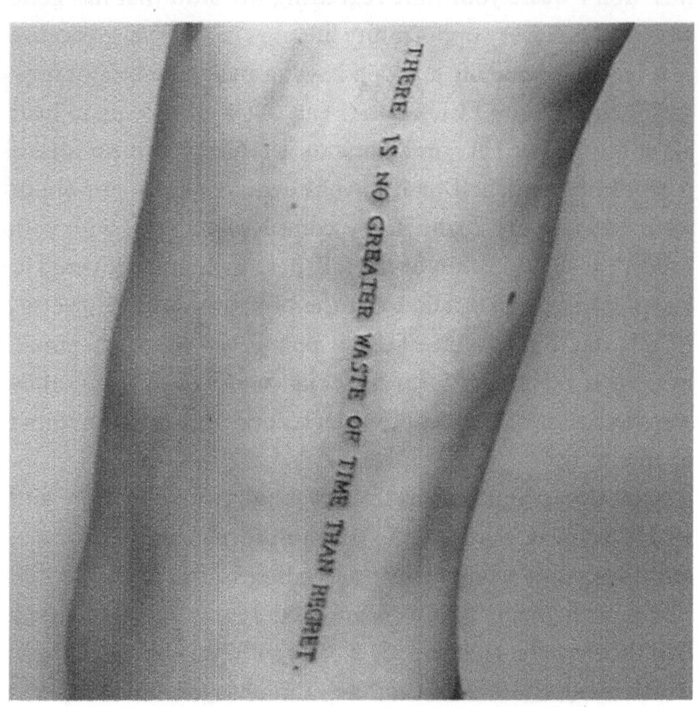

This is the young man who tattooed Mrs du Plessis's words of wisdom on his body so he wouldn't forget them. Let's hope he doesn't regret it . . .

or the fact that people are having "profound" life changes really comes down to me. It's all thanks to Mrs du Plessis.' I thought I would try to get in touch with her. It turned out to be easier to find her than I had thought it would be: she works as a child psychiatrist in Johannesburg now. We've been chatting and I've sent her the photo of the young man in Australia with the mantra 'there is no greater waste etc' (it doesn't say 'etc', but . . . you get it) tattooed on. I told her how she had changed my life, too, but probably wouldn't remember me. Teachers wouldn't, you'd think, as they have so many kids go through their class. But she remembered, and she also informed me that she was only a teacher for a very short time. In 1995, she went back to school to qualify as a psychiatrist, something she'd always wanted to do, and now she works with kids and teens who have had a traumatic life or who need guidance. Kids are truly her passion, and she's followed her heart and her talent and is now doing what she was clearly meant to be doing all along.

Later it hit me that I matriculated in 1994, and she went back to school in 1995. The odds of us meeting in order for her to utter those life-changing words to me were so slim, but it happened. Right place, right time? Everything happens for a reason? Who knows . . . What I do know is that if you keep your heart open, you will be blown away by the gifts — the experiences and the amazing people — you will receive in this life; this very, very short life that you need to grab with both hands like a sun-ripened mango and get stuck in. Who gives a shit if it's messy? Let the juice run down your arms and let your face get sticky! Enjoy the sweetness and suck all the juice off the pip. I love a good mango . . . I was just thinking mangoes, they're so expensive this season . . . Anyway. I digress. What I'm saying is: listen to other people and take their advice on board, because you will never live long enough to make all the mistakes necessary to acquire wisdom yourself.

*

I would hate you to get the impression that I now had life sorted, and all was roses and mood lighting. I still had the dipshit stepfather at home. When it comes to men, my mom only picks winners — not. Actually, Lettie has completely shit taste in men. Quintin, Reinette and I, with a bit of help from others, have worked out in recent years that out of the various kinds of romantic personality it is possible to be, my mother is a 'renovator'. She's one of those women who could never be satisfied with a normal, well-adjusted, functional and contributing man. She only picks men who need fixing up. That said, even she has come around to believing that a normal man would be worth a go, so if you're a normal man and you're reading or if you know one who's about Lettie's age, let's hook them up! My mother is one of the best people I know in the entire world and she deserves only the best, so I always say to her, 'If you can't find someone as fantastic as you, for Christ's sake, stay single. It's better to be alone and happy than with someone and miserable.' She's clearly come around to that point of view, too, because she's now been on her own for more than 20 years.

But it took a while, and in the meantime there was this dipshit stepfather. He was unemployed, and therefore at home all day. I didn't have much moral support at home any more. My brother had flunked out of school and had been called up for compulsory military training — as all white men at the age of 18 were in those days. My sister had dropped out of school as soon as she was allowed, had moved out, and was living three hours away with my aunty and grandmother doing a Girl Friday (secretarial) course and working in a mining town. I couldn't cope with my stepfather's company every day, so I made friends with an older lady who lived across the road from school. I used to see her gardening outside quite a lot, and got talking to her. It turned out her two youngest children — who she had in her forties — were in Hoërskool Brandwag, too. Her daughter Joylene was in my class, and we became very good friends. I spent most days after school at the old lady's place. I soon started calling her Ouma Wylie.

Ouma Wylie suffered from narcolepsy, which was always very entertaining. She would be sitting there, chatting and knitting and would fall asleep mid-sentence, only to wake up ten minutes later and just carry on with the conversation and keep knitting without missing a stitch. That always gave us a good laugh, but it also meant she very rarely left her house. She smoked like a chimney, and her husband (who treated her very badly) would only buy her a pack of tobacco and one pack of tailor-made cigarettes to last her a week. It's pretty hard chimney-smoking on that, so she would smoke it with a pipe, with the result that her grey hair had a permanent yellow nicotine stripe in it. I can't begin to recall how many times she fell asleep with that pipe lit, but there were burn marks all over her house and clothes. She was hands-down one of the nicest people on the earth. She never had a bad word to say about anyone, ever. I can picture her reading what I've written here and shaking her head over the fact I have pronounced people to be dipshits and assholes.

'Oh no, dear child,' she would tut-tut. I can just about hear her now.

**Ouma Wylie with a cigarette, holding it the wrong way.
She had just woken up.**

She was a very forgiving person. I sometimes wish I had an ounce of her capacity to forgive. But, then again, she wasn't a great advertisement for the wisdom of turning the other cheek: she was a doormat, and was walked over her entire life.

No one could ever accuse *me* of being a doormat! By now, I had a very combative relationship with my mother and my stepfather. Quite often I would march out of our house and go and live with Ouma Wylie for a stretch of up to a couple of weeks.

'Oh no, dear child,' Ouma Wylie would say. 'Ring your mother. She's doing her best and she's always going to be your mother. You won't always be this angry. Just try to be a bit kinder.'

She would explain that my mother had always been patient with me when I was a baby, and I owed it to her to be patient with her as a grown-up, because she always meant well. If I behaved as a little shit (not Ouma Wylie's words), I would regret it when I was older.

'If only I had one more day with my dear mother,' she would sigh. 'I'd spend it holding her hand and cherish it for the rest of my life.'

Well, bugger me if Ouma Wylie wasn't right! I didn't stay angry with my mother, although it took a while to stop. I don't always agree with Lettie, but I can see what a wonderful woman she is and, looking back, I can see how she always tried to do her best. I can still learn from her and, even if I have this policy about not wasting my time on regretting stuff, if I wasn't my mother's friend today I know I would regret it forever.

The One About
MY SHIP COMING IN

After I left school I was basically living my life like a fart floating around in the wind, to paraphrase Elton John. Actually, there's an idea for my funeral song! Sir Elton, if you're reading this and happen to outlive me . . . Anyway. There was no real direction in my life, I wasn't interested in anything, my mother couldn't afford to send me to university and getting a student loan was not an option. Even if it had been an option, I had no idea what I wanted to do with my life. At high school, I had got into drama and debating and I thoroughly enjoyed both. I got a scholarship of sorts to go study drama at the Academy of Drama and Art and I started doing that, more for lack of options than because I was a driven artist.

I had been there only three months when I happened to

hear that of all the people at the Academy, only one could expect to make it. Well, I wasn't by nature or conditioning the sort of person who would imagine that I was that One out of the 5000-odd people studying drama at the time. Nor was I content to be a struggling artist. By now, I was pretty over being poor. It's all fun and games in the beginning when you're being terribly creative and you're having fish and chips on a beach somewhere because you can't afford anything else because you're so busy being terribly fucking creative. But when that's your life, and especially when from time to time you can't even afford the fish and chips and you're having sandwiches on a beach, you'll be looking at the sunset and I can guarantee you won't be thinking, 'Woah. What an amazing sunset!' You'll be thinking, 'I wish I was having fish and chips' and, 'Why the fuck do I not have any money?' and, 'When the fuck will my ship come in?'

" NOR WAS I CONTENT TO BE A STRUGGLING ARTIST. BY NOW, I WAS PRETTY OVER BEING POOR. "

Now I don't know if that's an actual thing that people say: 'your ship comes in'. But my mother used to say it all the time to us kids when we'd ask for something.

'Mom, can I have a bike?'

'Sure, honey. As soon as my ship comes in.'

So even if there isn't an actual saying out there amongst the general population about ships coming in, please bear with me. And a warning. There might be other sayings in the book that you'll be reading here for the first time and I apologise for that in advance. I hope they'll be reasonably self-explanatory, but I did toy with the idea of including a sort of glossary at the back translating some of the more picturesque examples of stuff my family made up, or that I made up all by myself, or that I have simply misheard or mangled somewhere along the way so that it's entered my own private dialect of the English language. One that should definitely go in there is 'whatever tickles your fanny'. People hearing me say that probably laugh and wonder at the boundless creativity and limitless smuttiness of the professional comedian's mind, but honest to God, whenever I heard that saying growing up, that is what I heard. Apparently, that's not it!

“I DIDN'T WANT TO BE LIKE HER AND STRUGGLE THROUGH LIFE WORRYING ABOUT WHERE I WOULD GET MONEY FROM TO FEED MY KIDS.”

I found this out on a packed flight from Auckland to Queenstown. My wife made some remark to me and I replied quite loudly with my version of the saying and got one of the bigger laughs of my career in entertaining packed airliners. Only then did she correct me, although I had been saying it like that for years. That's how she rolls, see: she'll let me say stuff wrong for years because 'it's adorable' and then I'll say it wrong on TV or stage and she'll rush to slam the stable door shut long after we've watched the horse's ass receding into the hills.

Anyway, the point of the story is . . . ships! That's right! I spent a lot of time just after I left school scanning the horizon for that fucking ship, just like my mother had before me.

I didn't want to be like her and struggle through life worrying about where I would get money from to feed my kids — if I chose to have them, which, well, now I have. My mother seemed to have similar ambitions for me. The summer holidays were coming up and Mom told me to take a break from drama and find a seasonal job, because she wasn't going to support my cigarette-smoking and beer-swilling habits. So I grabbed the newspaper and applied for jobs, secretly hoping not to get them so I could just hang out with my friends playing indoor cricket, swigging beer and smoking cigarettes until someone tapped me on the shoulder and discreetly murmured that a ship had come in and the captain was searching everywhere for me.

I read that the local newspaper was looking for a typesetter. That sounded reasonably safe: I had no qualifications or relevant experience whatsoever, so the consequences of applying weren't likely to include any disruption to my holiday. I could hold my head up, look my mom in the eye and tell her that I had tried. That was the plan.

I rocked up to the newspaper and was directed to an office way down the end of a big open-plan space full of people driving computers amidst big piles of paper. I didn't even bother trying to picture myself in this environment. Nor did I imagine that one day the office on the door of which I was knocking would be mine.

Bisset Watson — how newspaper is *that*? — called me in. He was pretty brusque, and it was plain that lots of stress, booze and tobacco had gone into the creation of his leathery features.

'Can you type?' he asked.

'Yes,' I said.

'Can you spell?'

'Yes.'

He sat me down in front of a computer. I had learned to

type, but I had never so much as touched a computer before. He gave me an article from the paper, and told me to copy it as fast and as accurately as I could.

Well, I've got tiny hands, but, true as nuts, they can move pretty damn fast over a keyboard. Maybe Donald Trump could consider the typing pool when he's done with the US presidency. Anyway, I finished, and Bisset summoned a woman — Charlene Dowie, who became a good friend and who now lives in New Zealand — and got her to print the fruits of my labour. Bisset took it, frowned down at it, and then told me he'd be in touch.

A few days later, I got the call. I didn't get the job. Some girl called Debbie got it, and I was a close second.

So that was that. The beach was pretty nice, I was hitting the cricket ball pretty well and I was enjoying life with my friends, but a few months later I got another call. Bisset told me there had been a resignation and the job was mine, if I was available and still wanted it. Turns out that Debbie girl was a total fucking nightmare and nobody got on with her. Bisset was a 'take no prisoners, suffer no fools' kind of guy. He had put up with her for as long as he could.

The year was 1995. I reckon I am one of the last people on the planet to have done a typesetting apprenticeship! They trained me on the job, and I became proficient in the dark arts of assembling copy (written stuff) and images (pictorial stuff) into the pages of a newspaper. This was before the internet kicked in hardcore. We had to shoot 'negs' of each page in four colours: cyan(C), magenta(M), yellow(Y), and black (K — I don't know why it's K and not a B, either. I could google it, but I'll let you do it for yourself, while I go do it too. I'll see you back here in a second . . . K for Key. Very interesting). Then we'd send that along with an A3 printout of every page to the printer. So of course, if anything goes wrong or if a big story breaks — 9/11, or Princess Diana dies — then the paper gets pushed back and the print run is late and you will no longer be home — or starting your other job — by 6 pm.

I say 'other job', because from 1995 to 2005, I always had more than just one job. I worked bars, heavy-metal festivals, drag strips and I even worked as an indoor cricket umpire for a few months.

My main other job was as a waitress and bar lady at O'Hagan's Irish Pub in Benoni, where I worked with Reinette. The work wasn't that bad. It was a lot of running around and it was unpaid — you got your income from tips — but I'm not sure why it is that people seem to think that since you are working in service delivery, you must be earning roughly the same as, say, an anaesthetist. In my experience, I was treated worse in that waitress job than any other job I've ever done. It is no exaggeration to say I was treated like shit, or even a few degrees worse than shit. It was like someone stepped barefoot in shit on their wedding day while everyone was watching, so, instead of just wiping the shit off their foot, they have to make a whole fucking song and dance about it and ensure everyone sees that they have shit on their foot and aren't happy about it.

Luckily it's not the majority of people who treat wait staff like that. If it was, instances of people being beaten to death with an oversized pepper mill on a Friday would be much more frequent than they currently are.

I played a lot of indoor cricket — I am a batter, and I'm not afraid to catch a ball — and I got asked if I wanted a job as an umpire in my evenings off from the bar. So I would climb up little metal stairs and sit in a little metal cube and write down scores and take shit from drunk indoor cricket players all night for R75 — at today's exchange rate in 2019, it would be roughly $7.70. But I had to do it.

So that was my working week: up at 6.30 am Monday to Friday to start work at the newspaper at 7.30 am. On Mondays, Tuesdays and other odd days, I would finish at 6 pm, and umpire indoor cricket until late. Wednesday to Saturday, I would work at O'Hagan's from 7 pm till 2 am. And every Sunday I would work the bar at the drag races that were held at a deserted runway strip in Brakpan.

"BRAKPAN IS THE KIND OF TOWN THAT EVERY COUNTRY HAS, WHERE IF YOU WANT TO INSULT SOMEONE YOU SIMPLY ASK IF THEY ARE FROM THAT TOWN."

Brakpan is the kind of town that every country has, where if you want to insult someone you simply ask if they are from that town. Brakpan is such a shithole that just saying the name is like a swear word — I'm not going to win any fans saying so, but it's true. Of course, people from Brakpan don't believe they're bogans; they reckon bogans come from Danville, and they're right about that. There. Now I've pissed off most of the bogan population of South Africa.

Anyway. My job was to hand over drinks to people who were too drunk to walk but who were still going to race later that day. That's the joy of being a bar lady: you just hand it over and don't ask questions and pretend not to see anything. It was a very dusty place to work and, at the end of a very long day of noisy racing and serving drunk patrons, I'd have mud in every orifice. From my nostrils to my armpits, any spot on my body where moisture could accumulate would have turned into a little mud pit. I was covered in crap.

Now, I wasn't exactly going to become a millionaire working these three jobs, but there were valuable lessons in there for me. The main lesson that I took from it was to HANG IN THERE! It will all pay off in the end. I learned how important it is to work on your 'foundations'. I know it sounds weird, but whenever I go through a shit patch — by 'shit patch', I mean I do a shit gig or I work on a job that's time-consuming and doesn't pay and the client treats me like shit, or I'm in a festival where the festival director hates me because she can't be fucking bothered to get to know me (and most of them have a god complex like you can't believe) — I just look at my wife and say, this is 'foundation work'.

> ***"MY EARLY TWENTIES PASSED IN A BLUR OF LATE WORK AND HARD WORK, BUT I MADE FRIENDSHIPS WITH THE PEOPLE I WORKED WITH THAT WILL LAST A LIFETIME."***

Occasionally you have to push through a lot of shit to get to the gold. So when I worked as a waitress and bar lady I actually earned twice what I would earn at the newspaper in a month — still not a lot of money, around R4000 a month at the waitress/bar and R1500 at the newspaper, which is about $550 in total. Not a lot of money. Lots of people told me my investment in hours and energy versus the return I got did not add up, and advised me to quit the paper. But I knew I was working on my 'foundations' and that in the long run it would pay off. Of course, it eventually did.

*

For a 10-year period in my life, I didn't really have any time off, so guess what? Guess who did a whole lot of fucking and partying during that time? Well, I'm not sure, but I can tell you it sure as shit wasn't me. My early twenties passed in a blur of late work and hard work, but I made friendships with the people I worked with that will last a lifetime. I know it sounds corny as hell, but it's true. Even though I was tired a lot, I was young and always had a good laugh at work.

The One About MY NORMAL KIDNEY

When I was 20 years old, I started feeling weird, almost crowded inside my own body. To anyone who hasn't experienced it — which will be most of you — that will make no sense, but there is no other way to explain it. I remember going to my mother's house one night saying to her that I was convinced I was going to die in my sleep. I burst into tears and told her something was very wrong. She'd sort of got used to this kind of carry-on by now: I was all over the place like, as they say (or I think they say), a mad person's ship. I could go from completely calm to bat-shit crazy and absolutely weeping within minutes.

One day not long after I had announced my fear that I was going to die in my sleep, I was in a shop with Mom buying clothes. Now that's a stressful enough situation right there: buying clothes with your mother, especially given how much I hate trying things on. I am a very decisive clothes shopper. I see something I like and I just want to take it home. If it turns out my decision was in any way flawed or misguided, I have no qualms about bringing things back.

"I WAS CONVINCED I WAS GOING TO DIE IN MY SLEEP."

Anyway. This particular day, my mother was calling the shots. We'd found a prospective garment and, as usual, she insisted I try it on. So I walked over to the dressing rooms and there was a woman waiting outside. She was a bigger unit, wearing trackpants and the kind of Mickey Mouse T-shirt that was all the rage in South Africa in the early nineties. I expect it was supposed to depict a whistling Mickey Mouse taking a casual stroll, but because this woman was (as mentioned) built on a larger scale it looked like Mickey was attempting to hurdle a barrel and, from the expression on his face, was not too confident about the outcome. I locked eyes with this woman to sort of telepathically ask her if she was waiting for the changing rooms. She didn't acknowledge me, so I walked past her into the open changing room.

'Axcuse me, luydee,' she suddenly said in a very Afrikaner accent. 'Oi ken for loike to be waitings for thet chainging drooms!'

The normal, civilised response — and normally the normal me would just turn around and calmly deliver it — is: 'I'm sorry. I didn't realise there was a queue.'

Instead, I spun around and yelled right in her face.

'Just don't shit yourself, you fucking cow!'

Well, I don't know who was more shocked by what popped out of my mouth: me, her or my mother, who I could see out of the corner of my eye burrowing into a clothing rack. I have never forgotten the spectacle — and, in all my long years, I've never seen its equal — of a grown woman flinging herself under a clothes rack like that. I dropped the clothes I was holding and walked over to the clothes rack and said, 'Something is not right. I need to go see a doctor.'

The row of outsize Mickey Mouse T-shirts rustled affirmatively as my mother nodded in her hiding place. She crawled out, we went home and made an appointment.

The following Monday, I went and saw my GP. I told him I didn't feel great and he sent me off for some tests and scans — I could do those because I had a great medical aid scheme through work. In South Africa, medical aid is your personal responsibility, and without it you have to go to a state hospital. South African state hospitals are nothing like New Zealand public hospitals: you have to take your own bedding, food and cleaning stuff, and the standard of care is way lower. But happily, as it turned out, I had opted into the medical aid scheme that was my employer's preferred provider.

The scan results came back the same day and we were back in the doctor's surgery.

'Well, all the tests came back normal,' he said, 'except for an eleven-centimetre cyst on your right kidney. Nothing is out of the ordinary. You should be fine. Chances are it'll never bother you. Come back and see me in six months to a year and we'll do another scan and see how the kidney is doing.'

At this point I asked the doctor to back the fuck up.

A cyst, you say? Eleven centimetres? *Eleven* centimetres? Eleven *centimetres*? How's that normal?

'Oh, it's quite common.' He shrugged. 'You'd be surprised how many people are walking around happy as anything with eleven-centimetre cysts on various bits.'

For the record, since that day, having sought a second opinion and having told that story hundreds of times in my 'I'm going to need a second opinion' show, I've only ever heard of one other person who had anything like it. And as for it not bothering me? I went to see him in the first place *because* it was bothering me. I had been living with the unshakeable conviction that I was fighting something or other for the right to occupy my own body for months. Stop me if my imagination is running away with me, but maybe this *fucking enormous cyst* had something to do with that!

I left his rooms that day knowing two things. First, I needed a new doctor. Second, I needed a second opinion. Trouble was, the way even the private system was in South Africa in those days, you could only receive medical aid for a consultation with a specialist if you had been referred by your doctor. So, after doing some research which turned up a urologist living quite near my house, I rang my doctor and made him fax me a referral. (For younger players, the 'facsimile' or 'fax' is a primitive form of communication that works much like using a sandwich press to send a message to another, far-off sandwich press.) Two days later, I took my referral and marched over to the urologist with the images from my scans in hand.

'Now, what seems to be the problem?' he asked.

I told him that my doctor had found a cyst on my kidney but that he'd also said that it's quite common.

'Yes,' the urologist agreed. 'It is quite common. I see quite a lot of them, and usually they're completely harmless. I don't even bother to look at any scans unless the cyst is bigger than nine centimetres.'

I probably grinned grimly at him. I definitely told him to strap in, then I showed him my scans. He sat up, frowned, picked up the phone, and ordered more scans.

I was back in his office a few hours later.

'The cyst now seems to be nineteen point five centimetres in diameter,' he said.

I stared at him, doing the math. In two days that cyst had nearly doubled in size! I was in serious danger of being evicted from my own body!

He wasn't finished yet.

'Oh, and it's become septic,' he said. 'The matter has become urgent.'

I was admitted to hospital later that same day, and they wasted no time prepping me for surgery. Just before I went in, Ouma Wylie rang me. Whether it was because of her eyes or her narcolepsy, or whether it was because she was just afraid, she hardly ever left her house. She badly wanted to come to the hospital to see me, but just couldn't bring herself to do it. She read me a passage from the Bible over the phone and I could tell she was crying. I did my best to reassure her, and I was probably quite convincing, because I still didn't think it was very serious. I had what two doctors considered to be a common and pretty normal condition that had just got a bit too normal for comfort, and had turned slightly abnormal, all of which was probably pretty normal. I thought I would be under the knife for a couple of hours and then I would go home and go straight back to work, swilling beer and smoking cigarettes.

It took five hours, and they removed not only the cyst but also the kidney and the adrenal gland. Among other things, adrenal glands have a fair bit to do with controlling your hormones and therefore your moods. Mine was being squashed by the cyst and so my hormones were doing a bit of a Chernobyl in there, which may have accounted for my vicious mood swings. Under the circumstances, that cow with the Mickey Mouse T-shirt can thank her lucky stars I didn't rip her heart out and show it to her, still beating.

In the age of keyhole surgery, they can do amazing things inside you and leave only a tiny mark on your skin. I must have slightly pre-dated keyhole surgery, because I look like I got drunk and picked a sword fight with Zorro. I woke feeling incredibly sore. There was a nurse sitting beside me in the recovery room who smiled and patted my hand.

'Don't worry, love,' she said. 'The surgeon thinks he got all the cancer out. He'll come and talk to you when he does his rounds in four hours.'

'Oh, that's good,' I murmured woozily. 'They got all the . . . hang on! Cancer?! What the fuck?'

'Relax,' soothed the nurse, and I started to panic. Four hours is a long time to wait when you think there's a good chance that at the end of it they'll send you home to put your affairs in order. I don't think I've ever been that stressed in my life, other than the days my kids were born.

You can do a shit-load of thinking in four hours. My immediate thought was 'I need to come out of the closet.' Up to that point, I had been so comfortable with the knowledge that I was a lesbian that it had not been an issue for me that no one else really knew. Well, obviously, the people I was dating probably knew, but I didn't make a song and dance about it to the rest of the world, even though I had studied singing and dancing for a career for a while. But as I lay in hospital with, as it seemed, my life in the balance, I knew that I didn't want to be one of those closeted people who get married against their better sexual judgement and live a lie. We all know that one couple where you wonder, 'How can the other person not see what's going on?' Then there's the inevitable break-up and the tearful 'I never knew or suspected a thing' conversations, and you think, 'How did you *not* know?' I did not want to be the person another person had those conversations about.

"BUT AS I LAY IN HOSPITAL WITH, AS IT SEEMED, MY LIFE IN THE BALANCE, I KNEW THAT I DIDN'T WANT TO BE ONE OF THOSE CLOSETED PEOPLE WHO GET MARRIED AGAINST THEIR BETTER SEXUAL JUDGEMENT AND LIVE A LIE."

Yep. As soon as I got the good news, I decided, I was going to harden right up and start making some announcements to my friends and family.

The surgeon came in. I could hear my heart hammering, probably enjoying all the extra elbow room it suddenly had in there.

'It's good news.' He beamed, and went on to tell me that they removed everything suspicious and that the only downstream consequences I could expect were that they'd have to keep an eye on the area and monitor the function of my sole remaining kidney for the foreseeable future.

After 'good news', all I heard was 'blah blah blah'. I was thinking, 'Thank fuck for that. I won't have to tell anyone I'm gay just yet.'

The Whole APARTHEID ROUTINE

While all this was going on, people were leaving South Africa in droves. It seemed that, as fast as I could make friends (which wasn't very fast, but I did really like some of the people I did my apprenticeship with at work), they left and went to the UK. By the time I came out of hospital and began the recovery process, I swear to God my only friend within a 4000-mile radius was Ouma Wylie. It was, of course, that period in South Africa's history where apartheid was ending and people were terrified about what that meant for the future. Now I'm conscious that anyone who was grateful for my explanation of the concept of the fax will be hanging out for me to explain this little word 'apartheid'. So here goes.

Basically, the mostly Dutch Europeans who settled in South Africa from the seventeeth century onwards wanted to have the place to themselves. That meant kicking out the people who were already there — and there were quite a lot of African people already living there, and plenty more were arriving all the time from other parts of Africa. Kicking them out didn't altogether work, so a political system was devised that made sure that white people got the best bits of the country, and black people kept themselves to themselves. I know, it all sounds a bit strange — until you understand that God had told the white people that it was OK.

The word 'apartheid' means 'apartness', or 'separateness'. Racial segregation became official government policy in 1948, but that was just being formal about what successive white governments of South Africa had done their best to achieve for a couple of hundred years: dividing the country up so that everyone could live in peace and harmony without having to bother one another with arguments about whether it was actually fair that the whites got absolutely all the goodies.

Of course, that kind of argument happened anyway, and at times like these the white people tended to deal with it by being very violent. The year 1976 was notable not just for my birth, but also for one of the best-known examples of a protest against the apartheid system that was brutally repressed by the white government. For most of the time that the apartheid system was in place, the government had managed to keep the resistance movement swept under the rug, so to speak. Throughout the sixties, they had done a particularly good job of pretending to the rest of the world (and probably to themselves) that South Africa was some kind of split-level paradise, but all they really achieved was to keep the rage and anger bubbling away under the surface. As we all know, the way to really wind someone up is to control them: it's like slowly applying pressure to a pimple — eventually it's going to pop. In 1976 in Soweto (one of the bigger 'townships' that were built especially to house black people) a peaceful protest was held against the fact that everyone in school was being taught in Afrikaans, the language of the white government, who were also the oppressors. The number of students taking part in the march grew quickly to over 10,000. The police unsuccessfully tried to reason with the crowd with warning shots and tear gas. When that failed, they realised they would have to be more persuasive and opened fire straight into the crowd with live ammunition.

> **"CIVIL UNREST AND PROTEST WAS A CONSTANT THEME WHILE I WAS GROWING UP, AND SOUTH AFRICA WAS INCREASINGLY ISOLATED FROM THE REST OF THE WORLD."**

Two people — Hastings Ndlovu and Hector Pieterson — lost their lives; hundreds were injured and millions are scarred to this day because of what went down. There's a monument erected in Soweto on the spot where the pair were killed to remember that day. It was the worst moment of violence since 1960, when 69 people were massacred in similar circumstances at another township named Sharpeville. It was a very important day and marked a definite change — the end of the 'silent decade'. June 16 is now known as Youth Day in South Africa. When you see photos, you'll realise that even you know about that day.

Soweto sort of marked the beginning of the end for the apartheid regime. Civil unrest and protest was a constant theme while I was growing up, and South Africa was increasingly isolated from the rest of the world. The

A dying Hector Pieterson being carried by Mbuyisa Makhubo during the Soweto Uprising on 16 June 1976.

pressure was building all the time. In the end, all it took was for a schoolteacher from Mount Roskill in Auckland, New Zealand, to give the word, and it all came crashing down — but we'll come back to that later.

*

Some of the most hated measures in the whole hateful apartheid system were the Pass Laws, which meant that all black people had to carry a pass with them at all times to say who they were, where they lived and if they had permission to be in the white neighbourhoods. If they were caught in a white area without a pass, they'd be arrested and then God knows what. You weren't allowed to have black people stay over in your house; you weren't allowed to have a black man in your car if you were a white woman; you weren't allowed to have a black woman in the front seat of your car after a certain time of day . . . I can't remember all the rules. I just know it was all fucking ridiculous.

My mother was bitterly opposed to apartheid, and she often broke the rules. She would hide people in our home and swear us kids to silence. I knew from a very early age that if I didn't keep my mouth shut, people could get hurt. Now, I'm not talking about harbouring political prisoners or guerrilla fighters or people trying to overturn the government of the day; I'm simply talking about family members of the people who cleaned the train station where my mother worked. I'm talking about people who missed the last bus out of the white neighbourhood and would have got the shit kicked out of them if we didn't let them sleep in our sleep-out — most houses in South Africa had a sleep-out where the domestic would live. 'The domestic?' you ask. The maid. The help.

The servant. The slave. To this day, I don't know what to say to make that sound normal or acceptable. Even now, most households in South Africa have domestics who clean, help with the cooking (that is: do the cooking) and help raise the children. If you've ever seen the movie *The Help*, then you'll know exactly what I'm talking about. I watched that movie and wept for three days. It was quite emotional.

I'm not 100 per cent sure when I personally became aware of the political struggle in South Africa. I don't really know that I ever knew. Once in the car, we drove past a big CNA, which is a chain of stationery stores in South Africa. Quintin, who was always good at anagrams, asked my mother if it was a front for the ANC (African National Congress).

'No,' she replied, 'it's not.' The ANC had been pushed underground and they were illegal so they probably wouldn't be able to be so blatant as to sell a few staplers and pens and think that people wouldn't notice. My brother asked if Nelson Mandela was also pushed underground. My mother answered that yes, he was also 'underground', in the sense that his political views were locked in prison with him and he was not allowed to communicate with his followers.

That was the first time I can recall ever hearing about the ANC or Nelson Mandela. I couldn't have been more than eight at the time, and in my head I immediately pictured them as literally underground. For years, without question, I thought that the ANC was a political group that worked out of basements and complex tunnels running under Johannesburg. That, of course, wasn't true, but it wasn't totally wrong either!

I knew things were dangerous in South Africa and I was

aware of the bombings and that we had to be careful and not go near unmarked packages. For as long as I can remember, I had a plastic card on my suitcase with my name on it, where I went to school, my blood type, my address and mother's contact details. This was in case either my bag got left somewhere — they would be able to contact someone before they took the bag away and blew it up — or I got blown up, whereupon they would be able to identify me, give me the right blood and notify my next of kin. These days, of course, all the information I had on a card strapped to the outside of my bag would be absolutely everything you needed to take over my identity, if you felt so inclined.

"IF YOU GROW UP WITH IT, YOU DON'T KNOW ANY BETTER, SO I NEVER REALLY FELT UNSAFE OR EVEN AWARE OF THE DEEP DIVISION IN SOUTH AFRICAN SOCIETY."

If you grow up with it, you don't know any better, so I never really felt unsafe or even aware of the deep division in South African society. But I became very aware of it in 1988. I was 11 years old and in my last year of primary school when a bomb was planted in the Wimpy — a popular burger restaurant — in the plaza where we used to play after school. We had only ever gone to the Wimpy once in my life, when my grandmother visited and we shared some chips while she had a coffee. We were too poor otherwise, but we used to ride our bikes and play in the fountain in summer. We weren't supposed to play in the fountain, of course, but by now you'll have a fair idea of how much respect I have for rules. Sheesh. I'm glad I didn't raise me.

Anyway. One Saturday afternoon in July 1988, when the plaza and the burger restaurant were packed as usual, a limpet mine that had been stuck under one of the chairs went off, killing a 21-year-old woman and injuring nearly 60 people. It wasn't the first time I'd heard of a bombing and it sure as shit wasn't the first time someone had died in one of these guerrilla attacks that were happening all over the country, but it was the first time we were that close to it — in our town and in our Wimpy. We knew people who were injured in the blast. I knew what the chips tasted like there, and I wondered if that dead woman was eating them when . . . It scared me. A lot.

The One About
OUT OF AFRICA

The white government had introduced a number of reforms to try to soften apartheid during the eighties, but by 1990 it was clear that something had to give. In 1990, Nelson Mandela was released from prison.

I have always been a huge Nelson Mandela fan. When I look at what he did and what he gave up to do it, I'm moved to tears. I mean, I believe in things. I feel strongly about feeding hungry children and stopping animal abuse. But will I give up even a month without my wife and children to go and fight for those causes? No, I bloody won't! Mandela gave up 27 years to fight for a cause that he believed in — namely freedom for his children, freedom that he and his forefathers had never had. He gave up any chance of a normal life with his wife and kids, going to school events, soccer games, dance recitals, kids' birthday parties. Even when they offered to let him out if he told his comrades to stop fighting and killing, he chose to stay in prison. He would not accept freedom for himself until it was guaranteed for his all fellow South Africans. I think it's inspirational that anyone can put their own life second to the cause they believe in.

Now, I sense a few puzzled frowns out there. As incredible as it seems to me and to all South Africans that there could be people who don't know all about Nelson Mandela, I know you're out there. Your fax must have broken down the day they sent out the press releases.

> **"I THINK IT'S INSPIRATIONAL THAT ANYONE CAN PUT THEIR OWN LIFE SECOND TO THE CAUSE THEY BELIEVE IN."**

Whenever anyone has noted my accent and gone, 'So, like, South African, eh? Apartheid and all that . . .' I've responded by giving them a little quiz. I'll ask them why they think Nelson Mandela went to prison. The number of people who reckon it's because he was black is incredible!

Well, honestly, if that's what you believe, you need to read something. I'm not talking anything with too many words or pages, like a history book or anything, but maybe you could start with a woman's magazine and then slowly work your way up to the point where you can actually take in facts. In the meantime, I'll try to save you time and trouble and the need to read *Woman's Day*.

Pay close attention.

Nelson Mandela was head of the African National Congress, which started out as a political party. But for every step forward the ANC took the apartheid government would push them two steps back. It got to a point where Mandela realised that non-violent protest — the whole Gandhi approach of peace, respect and patience — wasn't working. How badly it wasn't working was brought home by the Sharpeville massacre, and soon after that Mandela established a military wing of the ANC called Umkhonto we Sizwe, which is 'Spear of the Nation' in the Zulu language. It was immediately classified as a terrorist organisation and banned in South Africa and in the US. It's all pretty standard stuff, and much the same kind of thing is happening all over the world today. After all, the militant wings of political movements are where the world gets all those terrorists you hear so much about.

When I tell people that Nelson Mandela was arrested and charged with high treason because he was a terrorist, they tend to react badly. If you're reading this and reacting badly, get your knickers out of your asshole. It's always been the case that one person's terrorist is another person's freedom fighter. I once said to a man in Melbourne that if Mandela was arrested and went on trial in the US today he'd be sitting on death row for being a terrorist. He looked at me very puzzled and smug at the same time — you know the look that your cat gives you when it runs into the house with a mouse and is standing there proudly and wondering why the fuck you're screaming your head off? Well, that's the look he gave me, and he simply said, 'It depends which state. Not all states in America have the death penalty . . .'

Fuck me. It's just impossible to help some people.

I say Mandela was a terrorist, but I understand what he did and why he did it. It was a struggle for freedom! People lost their lives on both sides of the fight. I'm sad for them and happy the fight is over. But I don't believe for a minute that South Africa would be where it is today without terrorism. Don't get me wrong, I'm just like everyone else — a peace-loving, non-violent, shy and retiring kind of soul. And, like everyone else, you just shouldn't fuck with us. Because we might turn the other cheek for a little while, but don't count on it indefinitely. Sooner or later, people have to fight if there is to be justice. After all, if a neighbour is oppressing your family, any member of it, even your mother-in-law — you'll take a harder line eventually. You'll stop mowing the little bit of grass verge that belongs to them. You'll start flipping dog shit over their fence, just so they know. They'll know! That's how people end up militant. That's where terrorists come from.

> **"SOONER OR LATER, PEOPLE HAVE TO FIGHT IF THERE IS TO BE JUSTICE."**

*

With Mandela out of prison at last in 1994, the first multi-racial government in South Africa's history was elected and apartheid was officially at an end. Everyone lived happily ever after. Not.

What you'll find is that it's quite hard to wipe away three hundred years' worth of gross injustice by grinning sheepishly and saying, 'Sorry. My bad.'

By the end, the idea that God had said it was all right hadn't quite concealed from Afrikaners — the descendants of the original white settlers — the fact that what they were doing was oppressing the black majority of South Africa. Most Afrikaners had worked out that black people were pretty pissed off about being oppressed, whatever God had said. You can understand why there was quite a lot of apprehension about what would happen next when the oppressed came knocking on the door of their former oppressors. Throughout the nineties, as I mentioned, Afrikaners were living in fear and leaving in droves.

> **"AFRICA GETS IN YOUR BLOOD. EVEN WITHOUT SEEING THE REST OF THE WORLD, I SORT OF KNEW THAT THERE'S JUST NO OTHER PLACE ON EARTH LIKE IT — NOT EVEN SIMILAR TO IT."**

I never had any desire to leave. South Africa was my home and I loved it. Africa gets in your blood. Even without seeing the rest of the world, I sort of knew that there's just no other place on earth like it — not even similar to it. You can't explain it. Nor can I easily explain my attitude to my heritage. Afrikaners to this day are regarded as the oppressors and there is a lot of hatred towards Afrikaans, which was the language spoken by the National Party, who were the architects of apartheid. In fact, so widely despised is Afrikaans that it is in danger of dying out. 'Good riddance,' you might think, but not everyone thinks that way about it. There is even a movement to teach it to our kids to keep it alive. Quite a few Afrikaner people don't take pride in their language because of all the baggage from the past. But I was born into an Afrikaner family. I still have family members who can't speak a lot of English. While I understand why Afrikaners and Afrikaans are fiercely hated, I am proud of my roots.

I suppose I can take this attitude because I grew up as a

A common sight in apartheid South Africa. There were 'whites only' everything — beaches, neighbourhoods, buses . . .

mostly white girl through the apartheid years and was on the lucky side of it. I say 'mostly white' because of all the haziness that there is over the precise details of my ancestry, and let's just say that I tan very easily . . . But it is also because I firmly believe that it will take all of us — white, coloured, black and potentially partially black — to put the past to rest and to move forward.

Did I ever see black people treated poorly? Yes. Have I ever seen a black person beaten simply because of the colour of their skin? Yes. Have I ever seen a black person lying dead in the street and not even respected in death because of the colour of their skin? Yes.

Have I ever seen a white person treated poorly? Yes. Have I ever seen a white person beaten simply because of the colour of their skin? Yes. Have I ever seen a white person lying dead in the street and not even respected in death because of the colour of their skin? Yes.

All I'm saying is that South Africa is a country with deep-rooted problems and it'll take several generations to sort it out. God knows I hope it gets sorted out. It's an amazing country. Its beauty knows no bounds and its people — when they aren't angry and killing each other — are the most amazing people in the world. You will not go unfed in Africa; you will not go there without receiving a warm welcome. But yes, there are a lot of problems.

To an extent, the fears of some of those who left in the nineties proved well founded. If you've ever read the statistics, you'll know that South Africa is a troubled place. It's riddled with crime and horribly high levels of unnecessary violence. But as my friends left (in droves, I think I mentioned) I stayed on and didn't even really question my decision to do so — until my best friend of them all left.

She didn't tell me, but when I went into hospital for my surgery Ouma Wylie already knew she was dying of cancer. She got pretty sick while I was recovering, and she died soon after I was well enough to be up and about.

"A LOT OF PEOPLE BELIEVE THAT, EVEN WHEN A LOVED ONE HAS 'PASSED OVER TO THE OTHER SIDE', THAT PERSON IS STILL WITH THEM. HUH! I'M ONE OF THOSE PEOPLE!"

I loved that woman so much. It was 1999 when she died, and I was 23 years old. Her death was (and is) one of the hardest things that I've ever gone through. A lot of people believe that, even when a loved one has 'passed over to the other side', that person is still with them. Huh! I'm one of those people! Even in my most cynical frames of mind — and, let me tell you, those frames can be pretty fucking cynical — I can't shake the feeling that Ouma Wylie is with me. Every now and again I'll get a whiff of the unmistakeable smell of pipe smoke — and, let's face it, who smokes a pipe in this day and age? That's when I know she's with me and it makes me happy. The things I remember most about her is she made the best ham and cheese toasted sandwiches and could nurse anyone back to health, because she had a heart of gold. Anyone but herself, that is; sadly she couldn't doctor herself, and nor could anyone else by the time she finally stopped looking after other people and worried about herself enough to go and see a doctor. She probably thought that whatever was ailing her was just her due. If I take anything from the manner of her death, it is that you should always look after yourself and put yourself first. If she'd done that, just for once in her life, she'd probably still be here. My wish is that everyone will experience the love and generosity of a woman like Ouma Wylie.

Her death knocked me around. I felt hollow and started

"MY WISH IS THAT EVERYONE WILL EXPERIENCE THE LOVE AND GENEROSITY OF A WOMAN LIKE OUMA WYLIE."

questioning everything. Why the hell are we here? If life is a journey, why does that journey end so shit? No one gets out alive — the last years of our lives are all the shit ones. We sit in our own filth and we struggle to do the basics for ourselves and if you're lucky you'll die in your sleep. If not, you'll probably break a hip in the park because some little asshole on a skateboard hit you while skating where they aren't supposed to and now, whatever you've achieved in your life, you're dead.

Then one night, while visiting my mom at her flat, I parked my little white-and-blue VW Golf outside on the street. When I came out after an hour, it was gone. I'd only had it a couple of years. I had bought it as a twenty-first birthday present to myself. It was my first car, my first major purchase of any description and, coming as soon as it did after Ouma Wylie's death, its theft felt as though the only thing I had left had been cruelly taken. I was inconsolable.

While I was filling out a complaint form for the police, the

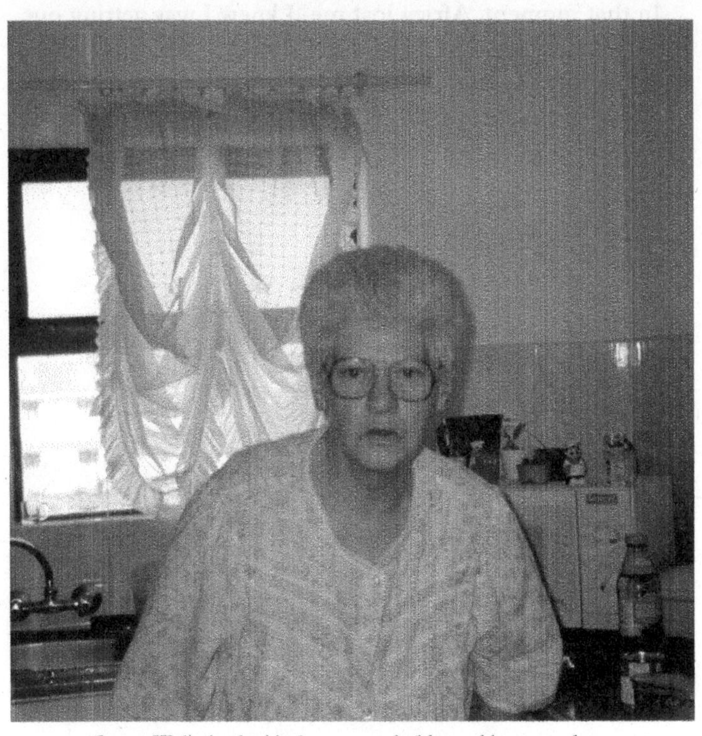

Ouma Wylie in the kitchen — probably making me a ham and cheese toasted sandwich. She passed away in 1999.

police officer asked me if I'd had the car stolen so I could get the insurance money. I was still paying off the car; I didn't stand to get any money out of the whole thing, even if the insurers did pay out.

In that moment, Africa lost me. I knew I was getting out.

The One About ME TAKING ORDERS

Once I'd made my decision, I didn't waste any time. I started looking the very next day for options that would get me overseas. I wanted to see America. I had no desire to go to the United Kingdom — never have — but I was keen to check out the States.

It so happened that in the course of my work that day I found myself typesetting an advertisement for au pairs to go to the US of A, and I thought, 'Yes! It's a sign!' If you were accepted, all you had to do was get yourself Stateside. They would cover your travel expenses after that, and, of course, you got paid, and meals and accommodation were taken care of.

Sold! That was me!

I called them immediately, and at their end the search was

on to match me with a family, while at my end the search was on for enough cash to fund my fare to the States. I didn't want anyone at work to know what I was planning, because, even though the pay was shitty, it was still money, so I didn't want to lose my job.

How to make money? Well, a fat girl sticks to what she knows. I made fudge! I made lots and lots of fudge and sold it door to door with a sign that said 'HELP ME GET THE FUCK OUT OF HERE.' I was worried people would look at that sign and sneer at me for the rat that I was, leaving a sinking ship. But, because of the political climate at the time, people saw my sign and bought the fudge and wished me luck and wanted me to let them know if I heard of a way they could get to leave, too. It was scary how many people were also looking around at South Africa and asking Scotty to beam them up.

Within a year — it might not sound like a long time, but it was hard slog and a lot of fudge went down — I had the money for my ticket. I got paired up with a family who were just about to move to Texas. The plan was that I would meet them in San Antonio, Texas. Brian and Jayne Allgood were a military family — they were both colonels — and they had only one child, a boy named Wyatt, who was four at the time. Now, I have to tell you, up to that point I had never lived with anyone other than my mother and my siblings in an in-the-house-and-in-your-face type scenario. Even at boarding school I had my own space and I could tell other girls to fuck off if they got up in my grill. So travelling to the other side of the world to live in a house with three strangers, two of whom were accustomed to working in a very structured environment, was no trivial matter. I'm pretty black and white in lots of my views — South Africans are big on monochrome, after all —

but not when it comes to my own issues. At that point, I want all parties to see things in greys, lots and lots of grey. Perhaps not quite 50 shades of it, but you get my point.

I found the militaristic nature of my host household challenging at times. Both colonels asked for stuff by issuing orders.

As for me, although I'm not about to start writing books on Modern Etiquette or anything, I do like the odd nicety here and there. I'm not great at taking orders. And rules? Meh. They have their place. It's just not necessarily my place. Jayne, the wife, in particular, had only two rules. Rule One: I am always right. Rule Two: In the unlikely event that I am wrong, refer to Rule One. It wasn't exactly a match made in heaven. She and I bumped heads quite a bit in the beginning.

> **"I'M NOT GREAT AT TAKING ORDERS. AND RULES? MEH. THEY HAVE THEIR PLACE. IT'S JUST NOT NECESSARILY MY PLACE."**

To make matters worse, the US military is not big on humour, and let's just say Jayne fitted right in there. I remember one bit of unpleasantness when I got back from a bit of a break in Washington, D.C. I was a bit gloomy, I suppose, and not as good at hiding it as I — or she, at least — would have liked.

'Are you sad because you're missing your friends?' she asked me.

'No,' I snapped back. 'I'm just missing being with normal people.'

Looking back, it's easy to see that I was struggling, missing my family, missing South Africa, and it was easier to lash out at this poor army woman who I was convinced had a touch of OCD than it was to admit I was doing it tough. I didn't cross swords with Brian quite so often, whether because he was always at work — he was an army surgeon and the Commanding Officer at Fort Sam Houston, which was near to where we were living just off-base — or because he, at least, was smart and funny. I was terribly sad to hear that he was killed in Afghanistan in 2007.

And I adored little Wyatt. We did everything together: we played soccer and went to the park and rode bikes and played blocks and cars and rolled around with the dogs and in summer we would swim for about three hours a day. He was a calm little dude, and he was super smart. One day, when my mother was over for a visit, she and I took him for a walk in his 'runner' — that's like a pushchair, but it is to the pushchair what a Hummer is to a Toyota Corolla. The Allgoods were a military family, after all, and they just got them bigger in Texas. Anyway. It was autumn, and all the leaves were doing what they do to inspire the Americans to call autumn 'fall'. 'Look at all the leaves!' Wyatt said to Mom, thrilled.

Mom, being a mom, said, 'Yes. Jesus put them on the ground for us to walk on like a carpet.'

There was a short, strained silence while Wyatt processed this.

'No,' he said. 'It's a seasonal thing, and I wouldn't be surprised if gravity plays a role.'

Mom and I just looked at each other and I laughed at her. She joined in because, well, what else can you do?

I was in Texas for 15 months, and I tried hard to settle into my new life. I spoke pretty good English, but a requirement of my visa was that I took an English as a Second Language

The Allgoods — Jayne, Brian and Wyatt.

Course that ran for an hour once a week at the local community college. Actually, my English was really good, and when the teacher's elderly mother got sick, they gave me an exam and then got me to teach the class. It was great! There were about eight of us in the class. There were Germans, South Americans and Russians. One Russian lady in particular — short, plump, in her fifties with a set of enormous, meaty hands — was amazing. She smiled at me a lot, even though we had very few words in common.

'Your family. Your mama,' she asked me after class one night, in a very thick Russian accent. 'Where . . .?'

'My mother lives in South Africa,' I replied.

'I cook for you,' she announced, and that was settled. From that day on, Martha (as she called herself in English) would bring a huge plate of cooked food for me whenever we had class. I loved the food, and I loved her!

I also studied history and maths. But I missed home and my family like anything. To try to keep the loneliness and the homesickness at bay, I cultivated links with South Africa. The trip I've just mentioned to Washington, D.C., was to visit Annesta and Etlane, who were also on the same au-pair scheme as me and who I had met in the queue at the US Embassy in Johannesburg. We'd kept in touch. They were in a similar situation to me: we were all young and away from home for the first time. We didn't want to go phoning our moms every other day, saying, 'I'm homesick! Help!' So we'd ring each other and say it. And there was a website I found for South Africans Living in Texas. I met Natasha through this, and we spent all our spare time together. Natasha had originally emigrated from South Africa to Germany with her mom, dad and sister, before moving on to Houston, Texas. She was married and wasn't working when I knew her, so

Me with Natasha Keyser, who I met on the website South Africans Living in Texas. We spent every moment together. We are still friends.

we spent all our free time together. I would drop Wyatt off at school and then immediately go and hang out with her till it was time to go and pick him up again. She and her husband had an apartment literally around the corner from the school, so it worked out really well. Natasha was three years younger than me, but she's an old soul, and she came across more like my mother, or a particularly maternal older sister, anyway. I came closest to coming out to her than I had with anyone ever before. I told her that I thought I might be bisexual — which was a far easier thing to say than to declare myself a lesbian!

My actual mother came to visit for five weeks roughly eight months into my time in Texas. It was a big deal for her: she had never been on a plane before, let alone left South Africa. She had moved ahead since our early days living in poverty. She had shed the deadshit stepfather, she now had a good job as head of the department in which she worked, she had downsized the house situation and was living in a two-bedroom apartment that was a lot cheaper than the house had been. Finally, it was as though her ship had come in. She had some money. We didn't spend lots when she came over: she stayed with me in my room and then we took a week and went to Corpus Christi, where we got a king room at the Ramada Inn for half price because they were renovating. We were used to doing stuff on a shoestring, so we had a cheap holiday, and walked so much that I thought my feet would fall off.

Mom still talks about it as the best holiday she ever had. It was definitely one of the nicest times of my life. We got on so well together, and it was amazing just watching her lapping up the different cultures and people interacting. I could see it was having the same effect on her — opening her mind, and making her more tolerant of ignorant assholes — as it was on me. So well did we get on that I seriously considered coming out to her. But something stopped me. I suppose it just didn't seem necessary, really.

The homesickness returned full bore when Mom left, but it sort of passed. I was beginning to feel settled in Texas. I dated a few people. I dated a boy who seemed to quite like me. I didn't realise quite how much he liked me until one evening, when we were in a movie theatre, he presented me with a ring that he had made out of paperclips and asked whether I would marry him. I let him put the ring on my finger, but I was suddenly scared, like when you think you're play-fighting with someone and then suddenly realise they're trying to kill you. Dating had never been a serious thing for me, but I remembered that other people took this stuff quite seriously, after all. I let him down as gently as I could, and vowed to myself that I would be more careful in the future.

When the colonels went on some kind of parent-visiting operation to Colorado to mark the turning of the millennium, Annesta and Etlane came down from Washington, D.C., to stay at my house, and we had a great time together. All of us were keen to do some more travelling. Our flights were all going through London, and we talked about maybe meeting up and extending our stopovers to do a bit of exploring.

When the time came, I left Texas with mixed feelings. It was good to be heading home, and exciting to be starting another leg of my adventure — even though there was a good chance it would be a stumpy little leg — and I was both happy and sad to be leaving the colonels and little Wyatt. Wyatt and I hugged and cried: he because I was going away and he wouldn't be reassured that I would see him again; me because, while I knew I would see him again, somehow I knew I would never see him again as a little boy.

I was nervous about what came next. Etlane and Annesta still seemed keen to meet up in London, but it was before everyone had a cell phone and the arrangement was kind of loose. We were flying to London from different parts of the US, and the idea was that they would be waiting for me when I walked out in transit. There would be no way of knowing until I got off the flight whether they were actually going to go through with it, or whether they would have changed their minds on the long-haul flight and decided to just head home. I wouldn't have blamed them.

What's more, I wasn't what you'd call a seasoned traveller by anyone's standards, so I was pretty anxious as I settled into my seat for the flight to Chicago, where I was to connect with the international flight to London.

Nothing much about that domestic flight soothed my anxieties. Somehow, the entire route from San Antonio to Chicago lay through this massive snowstorm. We flew all the way with the cabin lights off and the emergency lights on. The turbulence was so bad people were screaming and hurriedly converting to most of the world's major religions. We made it, but my nerves were shot to pieces. The flight to London was routine, but relaxation is hard enough in long-haul economy without the stresses and strains I had lately endured, so by the time I reached London I was in dire need of a cup of tea with a shot of something in it and a hug! I extended my ticket for four months and, with my heart in my mouth, I walked through into the arrivals area. For a moment, I couldn't see them, but then there they were: Annesta and Etlane! They had extended their tickets as agreed and we were together again in the United Kingdom.

We ordered drinks at a coffee shop and sat down. We looked at one another.

'What the hell do we do now?' I asked in Afrikaans, and they both shrugged. We hadn't planned any further ahead than this.

One of the other customers wandered over.

'You're speaking Afrikaans,' he said. 'You must be from South Africa.'

We replied that we were, and he said he had met a pack of three other crazy, drunk South Africans who were now living in Cardiff in Wales. He asked what our plans were.

We looked at one another and giggled uneasily.

'Not much, really,' we admitted.

So he rang the guys, and next thing we knew we were on a train to Cardiff.

SIX SOUTH AFRICANS, ONE SPANIARD AND THE WELSH . . .

We arrived in Cardiff in the late evening. It was cold and smelled strongly of coal, and its old, grimy brickwork was very different from all the shiny new glass and plastic stuff that I'd lived amidst in San Antonio and in the States in general. I felt kind of inclined to like it. The people looked smaller and poorer than Americans. We met our three new flatmates — Jan (pronounced 'Yarn') from Orkney, a little mining town in South Africa's North West province, Fred, who turned out to be Annesta's cousin, and another boy whose name I can't remember, because he got a girlfriend very shortly after that night — perhaps even that night — and soon moved out. They all seemed pretty laid-back and cool, and they had laid on a friend with a car who ferried us and our gear to the flat, a two-bedroom upstairs in a brick-and-tile walk-up. It was a pigsty!

We'd only just dumped our bags on the floor when our new flatmates announced they were on their way to a party, and asked if we'd like to tag along with them.

Sure, we shrugged.

The friend was a guy called Nathan (I can't remember his girlfriend's name) and they were lovely. When they heard about our situation — basically in transit in the UK for four months with no papers, no money and no plan to get some — they took us to a friend of theirs. Nancy was Spanish, and much older than the rest of us. She owned a pub, a proper Welsh pub, and we ended up hanging out there with our new friends most nights that we were in Cardiff. That first evening, I told Nancy how cool her nose ring was. She disappeared for a little bit and came back with an identical one — it was 18-carat gold with three little diamonds set in it — and presented it to me. I think I must have been a bit tipsy from the two bottles of South African Merlot on top of the long flight, but I received it with tears in my eyes.

'Thank you!' I sobbed. 'It looks just like Mickey Mouse!'

It didn't look like Mickey Mouse the next day, and it never has since. Drink has a lot to answer for. But I loved that nose ring. It sounds gross these days, but back then I used to think it looked as fab on me as its twin did on Nancy. I took it out as soon as I turned 30, because I didn't want to be one of those OLD ladies who wears inappropriate piercings. You can take the girl out of puritanical South Africa, it seems, but you can't take the puritanical South Africa out of the girl.

I sometimes think it's a shame this all happened in the time before Facebook, because I'm sure I'd be friends with those people and we'd still be in touch. But then, on the other hand, it's probably better that I just have my amazing memories and don't have to get annoyed at the volume of Candy Crush notifications I'd be receiving from them. So I'll keep them in the bubble that they occupy in my memory, where we are forever as cool as we were back then, when we used to sit about at Nancy's pub at 11 pm on a Monday night, smoking cigarettes and debating everything from politics to the best Syrah to drink and the competing merits of the wine regions of Spain versus Australia versus South Africa.

> **"YOU CAN TAKE THE GIRL OUT OF PURITANICAL SOUTH AFRICA, IT SEEMS, BUT YOU CAN'T TAKE THE PURITANICAL SOUTH AFRICA OUT OF THE GIRL."**

I don't think times like that exist anymore, not just because of (anti)social media, but because people now know how bad smoking is and most of us have kids. Try 9 pm on a Saturday and you might get something started, but it will never be the same as when we were young and free and invincible and altogether innocent of the horror of mixing a hangover with parenting small children.

Soon after arriving in Cardiff, I got a job through a contact of Nancy's, and — hold onto your good knickers — I worked in the Cardiff Bay Visitor Centre, which basically looks like a squeezed toilet roll. For this reason, it's known more or less affectionately as 'the Tube'. I worked there in the gift shop on Sundays and I helped out at the tourist information centre. Of course, I was a terrible choice to work there, because I had no idea where to send people. I tapped the side of my nose (where the nose ring was) and told them in my broad South African accent that, if they wanted an authentic Welsh experience, I knew just the place. Then I sent them for a feed and a drink at Nancy's pub.

I had fallen on my feet, and I met some amazing people in the four months I was there. But I'd be lying if I said it was all wonderful and I'd love to go back and do it all over again. We were working illegally, so we were definitely beggars rather than choosers. Besides the gift shop, I did bits and bobs of work in all sorts of different industries — everything from selling second-hand cars to working as a bar lady with Annesta and Etlane at this travelling heavy-metal festival. We poured a lot of beer for skinny people who — being Welsh — were not that tanned. We reckoned it was like an Addams family convention with a serious thirst on. The three of us had plenty of fun on this gig, but there were downsides. One of these was the weather, of course. Another was the UK's 'no pour' law, which stated you couldn't have a drink after 11 pm. This was a nightmare for those working in a bar: people would arrive, cock one eye at the clock and then binge drink until 11 pm, after which time they would be fucking pigs. But I can talk, can't I? More often than not, when I was on the other side of the bar, I was part of the problem. I drank heaps, and tipped my money down my throat as fast as I could earn it.

I do think the Welsh are, as a nation, way more aggressive than any other locals I've stumbled across. The six of us lived in the two bedrooms and we had to pre-purchase gas and electricity cards at the Spar, a convenience store just across the main road from our flat. One day, Annesta ducked out to get the cards. She was back within a couple of minutes — way too quick — and, seeing her face, I could tell she was spooked.

'What happened?' I asked.

'There were these two girls talking in the door of the Spar,' she replied. 'One of them had these really nice shoes on, and I sort of looked at the shoes and looked at her and was starting to tell her that they were really nice, and she goes, "What are you staring at? You got a problem? What's your fucking *problem*? Do you want your fucking head bashed in?"'

'So what did you say?' I asked.

'Nothing!' she said. 'I ran away and came back home!'

'Give me the money,' I told her.

I took the money out of her hand and set off for the Spar. The two girls were actually hanging around the entrance to our flat. As soon as I saw them, I locked eyes with them and yelled 'FUCK OFF' as loud and as aggressively as I could. I was obviously talking their language, stupid bullies, because they took off.

'Yeah,' I thought, watching them run. 'That's what you get when you mess with a woman who hasn't had a warm shower for two days because we've had to save up for the gas and electricity.'

Very aggressive people. There were a few incidents like that. I'm not sure if it can be attributed to the amount of alcohol they tend to consume, or if there's a drug problem or if people in Wales are just cranky because they don't get enough sun. The other example of what I'm talking about here was both scarier and funnier. We were pretty sure the people who lived downstairs from us were drug dealers. I have no proof, but they were like the movie stereotype of dodgy neighbours. They were a scrawny young couple who had a baby that screamed all hours of the day and night, and their apartment had a constant stream of shifty-looking visitors. All they needed to complete the picture was a rabid dog.

One day, they had a party, and some of the guests were vomiting on our stairs. Jan went down to have a word to them about it. Around 3 am, there was a godawful crash and a brick came through the lounge window. Two of the boys were sleeping in there — space was at a bit of a premium — and they were up and ready for anything else that might come through the window. There was a flickering orange glare outside and another crash of glass. The boys looked out to see the neighbours legging it, and smoke coming out of the broken window downstairs.

We all got dressed and ran down the stairs. We could hear the baby screaming inside, so Fred kicked down the door and set about putting out the fire that was blazing next to a broken window while Jan rescued the baby. By the time the police and the fire brigade showed up, Fred had put the fire out and we were back in our own flat with the scrawny little baby boy, who we handed over to the police.

We had sort of worked out what had happened. They had thrown the brick through the window so that they could follow it up with a Molotov cocktail.

First the 'fax', I hear you sigh. Now this 'Molotov cocktail'?

A Molotov cocktail (*noun*) is a crude incendiary device typically consisting of a bottle filled with flammable liquid and supplied with a means of ignition. A bottle of petrol with a petrol-soaked rag in it, set alight. And this is what they had tried to throw through the window of the flat above the one they lived in, and which they shared with their baby! Their elaborate revenge plot doesn't seem to have stretched beyond the point where they set the building on fire. And, in the event, whichever of them it was who threw the Molotov cocktail wasn't as good as the brick-thrower (that, or the brick was just a fluke), because the crude incendiary device had gone through the window of their own flat. Naturally, they had felt a bit anxious at this turn of events and run off.

Aggressive people, as you see. And not exactly criminal masterminds, or devoted parents either.

As it turned out, no harm was done. Everyone, including the baby, survived. The flat needed a new door and window and there was some smoke damage and the lingering smell of petrol. But those neighbours moved out the next morning, anyway.

Aggression? Drugs? Booze? The constant shitty, shitty weather? Who knows, but I saw plenty of it during my four-month stay in Wales. By the time those four months were up, I'd had enough. I wanted to go home.

I had been away from home for 20 months. It was a long time, especially given it was the first time, and I missed my mom and the rest of my family. Annesta and Etlane felt the same. We all hopped on a train and went back to London to go home. When I got to Heathrow airport, my bags were too heavy for the flight. It's a trap, you see: in the US at the time, you were allowed two bags and there was no weight limit, so of course, I had those puppies packed up the wazoo! But leaving the UK, there was a 23-kilogram limit. Well, that was my hand luggage! The excess-baggage charges were going to be something like £1000, and I didn't have anything like that kind of money, or any other kind of money, for that matter. I didn't want to get into a thing; I simply told them to phone the Red Cross and tell them I had a donation for them.

Annesta, who had fallen into the same trap but who is quite feisty, decided to put up a fight at the counter. They weren't having a bar of it and bumped both her and Etlane off my flight. That scared the shit out of me. It wasn't that I was afraid of flying home alone. It's just that Etlane and Annesta shared a star sign, and their horoscope for the day had advised that 'today

Me and all of the clothes that I left behind in Heathrow for the Red Cross. It's amazing how liberating it is to get on a plane carrying only the clothes on your back.

is a good day to travel'. I had consulted my own horoscope, and it had said, 'If you are planning to travel today, DON'T. Nothing good will come of it.' I'm very superstitious, you see, and I thought, 'Uh-oh! I'm dying in a fiery plane crash today!'

To cut a long story short, I didn't, and I wonder whether they got my horoscope mixed up with theirs. I survived that flight, and despite all the clothes and stuff I left behind at the airport — I arrived back in South Africa with photos and a few mementoes and not a lot else — plenty good came of travelling that day. I was home! Lettie and Quintin picked me up at the airport (Reinette had moved away to Cape Town) and I've never been so happy to see anyone.

'How was it?' they asked me as I settled into the car.

'Amazing,' I said, and I meant it. Not everything that had happened to me was great, but all of the experiences I'd had,

"IT WAS ONE OF THE MOST ENRICHING THINGS I'VE EVER DONE IN MY LIFE. IT MADE ME FEARLESS AND IT DEFINITELY MADE ME INTO THE WOMAN I AM TODAY."

good and bad, were mine and mine alone. It was one of the most enriching things I've ever done in my life. It made me fearless and it definitely made me into the woman I am today.

I opened my mouth to start telling them all about it. Where to begin?

'It was amazing,' I said again, and left it at that.

The One About SETTLING RIGHT BACK IN

I was back home in my beloved South Africa but, while I was enriched in spirit, the same could not be said for my material circumstances. I was broke.

I went back to the newspaper office to say hello to everyone and to Bisset Watson.

'Hope you enjoyed your holiday,' Bisset said. 'See you on Monday.'

I'd be gone for nearly two years. I laughed, he smiled, but the following Monday morning, I was snoozing comfortably at Mom's place, listening to the sounds of the rest of the world trudging off to work, when the phone rang.

'Urzy! It's for you,' Mom called.

'Hello?' I said groggily into the receiver.

'This is a great start back,' Bisset growled. 'You're late. Get your fat ass in here now!'

He was a newspaper man, see, so he had a way with words.

So I was back. And by midday on Tuesday, it was as though I had never been away.

*

But not for long, as it turned out. In 2002, Bisset called me into his office and told me that they had decided to make me his second-in-command.

He must have seen my face.

'What?' he said.

I was scared, I told him, and I was conscious that there were people who had worked there for more than 20 years who were only hanging in there because they knew he was approaching retirement and they were eyeing up his job. Some of them were openly talking as though they had already been tipped a wink by management. These people would deeply resent me, a 24-year-old, leap-frogging them on the career ladder, and would make my life hell if I started dishing out orders and setting deadlines.

Still, I'm no fool. I had no aspirations to be a manager myself, but I sure as hell wasn't going to turn down a promotion, either. So we agreed that I would take the job but that we would ease me into it so that both I and the old-schoolers had time to adjust. Bisset assured me he had my back and that he would deal with all the hate and acrimony and I could just learn the job. That gave me confidence, and Karen, the branch manager, announced my promotion at a meeting that day. The temperature in the room dropped by about 20 degrees, but

I didn't care. I was prepared to work hard and I wasn't there to make friends. I was there to succeed! I had the support of Bisset and Karen and I was up for it.

Two days after announcing my promotion, Bisset had a massive heart attack. I don't think there was any connection. I don't think he woke up and thought, 'Christ! What have I done? Carlson in a position of authority?' As I've said, he was a hard newspaper guy all his life, and chain-smoking, heavy drinking and long hours were all part of the hard newspaper guy job description. It all takes its toll. He nearly died. He had a quadruple bypass, took early retirement and never returned to work.

There was no on-the-job-training, and there was none of the softly-softly transition period we had planned. Bisset wasn't there to watch my back, after all, so I had to eat shit for a good few months before they came round to seeing and doing things my way without scowling and muttering. It was the toughest time of my life. A few times after everyone had gone home, I'd be alone in the office, and I'd just sit there grappling with the enormity of it all and fighting to hold back the tears. I knew that if I caved and started to cry, I wouldn't cope now, and maybe never would. I think that's the closest I've ever been to a nervous breakdown. I've never felt more alone in all my life, but I kept reminding myself what my grandmother — Ouma Ous, my real one, Mom's mom — used to say: the highest trees get the most wind. That hard old bitch was right!

I sort of modelled my managerial style on my grandmother's, who had modelled hers on other forceful managers in history, like Stalin, I suppose, or Genghis Khan. I was a steamroller. You were either going my way, or you got the fuck out of it if you didn't want to get squashed. I didn't take an ounce of shit.

While you wouldn't necessarily have known it from looking at the way things were done at Caxton, the business of putting newspapers together had changed in the last few years. We were still manually setting pages by typing text up then placing it using wax strips. This stuff is all done automatically in the age of computers. I made it my mission to bring us into the new millennium. Not everyone was 100 per cent behind me on this. In fact, the phrase 'kicking and screaming' comes to mind.

"I SORT OF MODELLED MY MANAGERIAL STYLE ON MY GRANDMOTHER'S, WHO HAD MODELLED HERS ON OTHER FORCEFUL MANAGERS IN HISTORY, LIKE STALIN, I SUPPOSE, OR GENGHIS KHAN."

'I've been here for twenty years!' some of the old hands would cry. 'I know what I'm doing!'

I would smile sweetly. Well, I probably didn't smile that sweetly. Actually, I probably fixed them with a death stare and pointed out that there were more streamlined ways of doing what they were doing. And that they had learned to do things their way on their very first day on the job and had just doggedly repeated it, day after day.

'That's not twenty years' experience,' I'd say. 'That's one day's experience repeated over and over for twenty years!'

It's lucky it wasn't a popularity contest. But little by little, as they realised that my way was actually quicker and easier and they got home while there was still sunshine in the day, they came around. I left the company in June 2006, and I reckon I left my department in way better shape than I found it.

Bisset didn't live much beyond a year after his retirement. Most of the guys I worked with back then have all passed away already. Not one of them made it to 65.

THERE'S THIS GIRL IN A CLOSET, RIGHT . . .

I am a firm believer that you have to be true to yourself. I had been seeing girls for ages. There was nothing ideological about my sexual preferences; I had just taken the approach that if I liked a person I'd date them. I didn't bother too much about gender. As I've mentioned, I had no intention of ever pretending I was straight just so I could live in the semblance of a 'normal' relationship. But the whole paperclips and proposal routine in Texas had woken me up to the fact that guys are people too. They have feelings all of their own, and hopes, and dreams, and it isn't fair to fuck with them. And I know it's a very competitive market and straight single ladies need all the players who aren't serious to move out of the way so they can find a man and settle down. I didn't want to be part of that obstacle course for a second longer than I needed to be!

What I'm saying is that, by the time I had been back in South Africa for a few months, I was just about ready to own the lesbyterian thing and remove myself from the straight market.

"WE'VE ALWAYS BEEN SO VERY CLOSE. NOTHING HAS EVER BEEN OFF LIMITS AND WE DON'T DILLY-DALLY; WE JUST FLOP OUR SHIT OUT AND TALK ABOUT WHATEVER IS ON OUR MINDS."

Telling my mother — even thinking about telling her — became a big thing. It never seemed like the right time, or the right place, or the right combination of time and place. But at the same time, I knew if I waited for the stars to align I'd never get around to telling her, so I thought I would bite the bullet and kind of lock both of us in on 'The Talk'. A garden nursery had just opened nearby. She loves nurseries; I said we should go to the nursery and have lunch, because I had something important to tell her.

We've always been so very close. Nothing has ever been off limits and we don't dilly-dally; we just flop our shit out and talk about whatever is on our minds. As soon as the 'something important' passed my lips, I knew that she would know what was coming. Still, I don't think I've ever been as nervous as I was on the day.

I picked her up from her house and I drove us to the nursery. We bought way too much stuff for the garden, because the entire time I was procrastinating and she was talking bullshit, both of us aware that we were avoiding 'The Talk'. We went into the café with dread dogging our footsteps and had lunch — a three-course meal — in just about complete silence. Then we left. We've never had so little to say to each other — nor bought so many fucking plants.

Mom seized the initiative. These days, she was working for our local vet — Doctor Andy — as a vet assistant/receptionist/holder of weepy owners and cat-pill inserter. She was really good friends with Doctor Andy. She phoned me one day a few days after The Silent Lunch, and the conversation went much like this.

'Urzy, you know Doctor Andy?'

'Well, yeah. Of course.'

'Did you know that one of his sons is gay?'

I thought I could see where she was going with this, but I played it with a straight bat.

'Well, no. I have no way of knowing that, do I?'

'Did you know that *Doctor Andy* knows?'

'No. Again, it's basically impossible for me to know what goes on in their house . . .'

'Do you know *how* Doctor Andy knows that his son is gay?'

'I shudder to think, Ma.'

'Don't be disgusting! Do you know?'

'No.'

'Doctor Andy's son simply gave Doctor Andy a call and said, "Hey, I'm gay." And now he's gay!'

'I'm pretty sure that it would have taken more than just that one phone call to make him gay.'

Mom dismissed this point as mere quibbling. She had her eyes on the prize. She pressed on remorselessly.

'I think it's great!' she enthused. 'You know, if I ever had to get a call like that from any one of my kids, I wouldn't mind. I would be proud — you know, if any one of you kids told me that over the phone . . .'

'Like, your only child who's not married and doesn't have kids? Like, that child?'

'Yes!' cried Mom, delighted I was catching on. 'Like, that child!'

'OK . . .' I said dubiously.

'Like, say, tomorrow morning at 7 am. If I came to work an hour earlier than usual and I had to get that call, then, well, that would be OK. That would be great! At 7 am.'

'OK . . .'

I got a text from my mother at 7 am the following morning, saying she was at work — which was strange, because that was an hour earlier than usual — and she was ready for her day. She was ready for anything. She was ready for her phone call.

I waited till 7.15. I knew that would drive her nuts.

Then I rang.

'Hi, Ma. I'm . . .'

'I KNEW IT!' I had to hold the phone away from my ear. 'WHY DIDN'T YOU TELL ME YEARS AGO?'

That was my entire 'coming out'. I know I'm very lucky. You do hear horror stories of how it is for other people — kids getting chucked out of home, or ceremonially struck off the Christmas card list, or disinherited and families ripped apart and so on. It wasn't traumatic for me and it wasn't even that life-changing. I told more people, because once you tell one person, it's like a portion of the riverbank breaking: it all just crumbles and falls apart and everyone knows. But the funny thing is — and I am professionally trained to recognise funny things — nobody was surprised. They all knew or had suspected for years, anyway. Of course, there was the odd person who reacted in a less-than-positive way, but I just gave them some space. There was no end to the amount of space I was prepared to give them. Some of them got their heads around it and came back. Some got the fuck out of my life, and good riddance to stupid shit.

> **"I'M NOT A GAY. I'M NOT A HOMOSEXUAL. I'M NOT PURELY A LESBYTERIAN."**

How does it happen, that people change their opinion of their child on the basis of their choice of partner? To me, the equivalent would be disowning your child because you dislike their partner. What if — God forbid — their partner is unattractive: do you disown your child because your grandkids will be ugly? What if their partner isn't the right religion or colour? Are you the same asshole who will disown your child then? If so, you need to take a good hard look at yourself. You're probably feeling pretty alone now that society has left that kind of Neanderthal thinking behind. It must suck big time. But look at it from the perspective of the person you rejected. They are far better off alone than with a family or a circle of friends who don't embrace them for the person they are. In the unlikely event you *are* someone who stopped talking to someone you knew for years and years who came out, just because you couldn't be arsed working through the biggest transition in their life (*their* life, not yours), then shame on you. Pick up your phone right now and make it right.

I seem to be on my soapbox, so why stop with the myth-busting now?

First thing to get straight — if you'll pardon the term — is that I'm not a gay. I'm not a homosexual. I'm not purely a lesbyterian. All of those things are just ways of describing how I identify sexually. That's not who I am as a person. A friend of mine used to say that straight people don't identify themselves by their husband or wife's name: if you are married to John, you don't walk up and say, 'Hi, I'm John.' So if you introduce yourself by saying, 'I'm gay', you are cheapening who you are, you are cheating yourself out of everything else that you also are. My favourite colours are green, orange and brown, but no one (least of all me) has ever identified me solely with my colour preferences. I've never been classed as 'the girl who likes autumn colours too much'. Like colour preference, gayness is a description, not a personality type. Call me simplistic, but I believe that sexuality is who you fuck, not who you are.

"CALL ME SIMPLISTIC, BUT I BELIEVE THAT SEXUALITY IS WHO YOU FUCK, NOT WHO YOU ARE."

People have asked me many times, 'When did you *know*? When did you know that you were gay?' Honestly, I don't think I ever thought any differently than I do now. It wasn't some kind of epiphany, something that dawned on me one day while I was, say, eating mussels — 'Hang on a minute! This is much better than last week's sausage sizzle!' I just always knew that one day I'd probably have a wife, not a husband. I never even for a second thought about telling my mother that I'm more attracted to women than I am to men. Why would I? She's never said anything to me about her preferences and, as far as I know, my siblings have never said anything to her, either. It all sounded so ridiculous, and just the fact that I now had to identify as a LESBIAN was something so weird to me. I couldn't even say the word LESBIAN, with or without capital letters, without laughing at myself!

But, despite all this, it's painfully obvious that the fact I am a lesbian makes other people feel awkward. I'm not exaggerating when I say that at least once a week a woman will walk up to me and say, 'I love you but I'm not a lesbian!' and then bray with uncomfortable laughter. Men will say, 'I love you — but you leave my wife alone!' and then always with the laughter. What do they think will happen? Do they think coming out as a lesbian is like being bitten by a fucking vampire, so that I now just go around compulsively (and indiscriminately) fucking women, any woman, even your drunk, middle-aged, overweight, unattractive wife? Er, no thanks. You got her, you keep her. I'm good. Gay people aren't put on this planet to fuck you or your spouse; we have our own wives and husbands and, trust me, when we're looking for someone it's probably not you if you're the type to think all we want is you.

I find it fascinating that some men will flat out refuse to go to a gay bar with a gay friend. Oh, so you're afraid someone will come on to you? Well, buddy, you need to check yourself because nine times out of 10, it's the fat, balding, broke blokes who are the most petrified of being chatted up. Here's the news I think you've been waiting for. Gay guys have standards and your unattractive, insecure broke ass does not fit the bill. Relax! You will get less action in a gay bar than you will in a straight bar, because gay people go into straight bars all the time. And lastly, let me tell you, I've never had people find out that I prefer women and all of a sudden it starts raining pussy on me! Calm down!

Right. So much for the straight people. I also want to spare a word for some gays who use their 'gayness' to indulge in really shit behaviour and then yell 'discrimination!' when someone gives them shit for their bad behaviour. I've heard close friends say to people, 'You're being a shit to me because I'm gay!' I've had to disabuse them. 'No, they weren't. They were being a shit to you because you were being a total asshole.'

> **"I'M ALWAYS A BIT AMAZED HOW WE, AS GROWN-ASS ADULTS, CAN TREAT EACH OTHER BADLY AND NOT TAKE RESPONSIBILITY FOR OUR OWN SHIT."**

I'm always a bit amazed how we, as grown-ass adults, can treat each other badly and not take responsibility for our own shit. We expect that of kids, but all too often we also tolerate it in adults. Quite frankly, that's why we have assholes like Donald Trump being president in the United States — because being a dick is considered OK and even, in some arenas, applauded!

Here endeth the lesbyterian lesson.

The One About OUT OF AFRICA ALL OVER AGAIN

In 2005, I bought a two-bedroom townhouse. I was in a relationship, by now. Barbara was eight years older than me, and she had a boy who was six at the time we met. She owned her own catering company back then and did very well out of it. She was — still is — into spiritual things, and she used to do a lot of courses in motivational stuff and things like Reiki. Let's just say that if there is a spiritual festival somewhere, Barbara will be there. I don't know who the father of her boy was. I never met him, I wasn't curious about him and Barbara seemed to have fully moved on from him.

I was at her house one evening, quite early on in our relationship, when her sister's teenage daughter rang and asked if we could take her mother to the doctor. My car was parked in the driveway behind Barbara's, so it made sense to take my car. We picked her sister up. We didn't know what was wrong with her, but she wasn't looking too good. While she was sitting in the passenger's seat next to me as I drove, she had a few of what appeared to be convulsions. Barbara was sitting in the back seat holding her shoulders and telling her she was going to be OK, but every time I caught her eye in the rear-view mirror I could tell she was as worried as I was.

When we got her to the doctor's surgery we dragged the poor woman out, slung an arm each over our shoulders and sort of marched her into the surgery. She was conscious at that point, but not for long, and she stopped breathing and went quite blue soon after we got her inside. They started doing CPR immediately and phoned for an ambulance. An emergency paramedic arrived just ahead of the ambulance, and they both parked right behind each other in a narrow little alleyway behind where my car was parked at the front door.

The ambulance driver had left the engine running, and someone passing by noticed that there was liquid dripping underneath it that looked and smelled like diesel. They turned it off.

All this time, I was outside, leaning on my car and smoking and trying not to worry about Barbara and what was going on inside. After almost an hour, the ambulance driver walked outside looking tired and sweaty. She noticed the ambulance was no longer running and asked if it had stopped by itself.

'No,' I said. 'Someone was worried there was a fuel leak and turned it off.'

'Oh no,' she groaned. 'The starter doesn't work, so we have to keep it running.'

'Shit!' I said, beginning to panic about how we would

get Barbara's sister to the hospital. 'Come on. We can push it out of the way and they can drive her to hospital in the paramedic's car.'

The ambulance driver didn't move. She looked at me.

'Are you related to the patient?' she asked.

'Yes, I'm her sister-in-law,' I replied.

'The patient is dead,' she said very quietly.

> **"IT WAS MY FIRST — AND I'M HAPPY TO SAY ONLY — EXPERIENCE OF SOMEONE DYING. THERE ONE MINUTE AND DEAD THE NEXT. I CAN REMEMBER IT LIKE IT WAS YESTERDAY, AND I STILL FEEL THE SAME SENSE OF PURE DISBELIEF."**

I couldn't process it. All I could think about was Barbara, and that I hadn't seen her for a while. I ran inside and found her just walking around like a zombie. It was my first — and I'm happy to say only — experience of someone dying. There one minute and dead the next. I can remember it like it was yesterday, and I still feel the same sense of pure disbelief.

The medics told us that Ansie had suffered a series of heart attacks in the minutes leading up to her arrival at the doctor's surgery. I think, deep down, I knew what was going on in the car, and I think I knew she was gone before we got her to the doctor. But it was surreal and terrible.

*

My relationship with Barbara was always rocky. We weren't that compatible, and we fought quite a lot. But sharing the awful death of her sister and then afterwards sorting out her affairs brought us closer together and, in retrospect, papered over some pretty big cracks. Otherwise, I think we would have broken up sooner, which would have been easier on both of us.

Instead, she and the boy moved in with me, and we started planning our future together. We were already thinking about emigrating, although we were keeping it quiet. Some of my friends — I'm looking at you, Mom — had made me promise that I wouldn't make any plans to leave the country again without telling them, but I had been planning in secret. I don't know what my reluctance is to tell people about major decisions. I suppose it's that feeling you get when they start trying to argue with you about what's best for you and your family, as though as soon as you start thinking big you have to negotiate your life with other people.

"I COULD DO MY BEST AND MAKE SURE I WASN'T PERSONALLY GUILTY OF ANY OF THE THINGS SLOWLY DESTROYING THE COUNTRY, BUT IN THE END I WASN'T GOING TO BE A VICTIM OF IT."

Also, with people leaving (yeah, in droves), there was a certain touchiness amongst those who were left. They made you feel like a traitor for even considering leaving, when it was clear to them that an Afrikaner's duty was to stay and stick it out and help fix the problem. Well, I never signed up for the military. It's not my job to fight for South Africa. It's not my job to sort out the violence and crime in the country and the breakdown in the delivery of basic services. I could do my best and make sure I wasn't personally guilty of any of the things slowly destroying the country, but in the end I wasn't going to be a victim of it.

And last of all (OK, I know, sounding a bit defensive here) if people only have to deal with the shock of you leaving, it works better. People don't get resentful because you're planning on leaving; they just start missing you immediately, and you can skip all those tedious months of arguing and bad feelings that arise because you've told them you're planning something that will mean they won't see you twice a year like usual.

Of course, not everyone is like that, and I told some friends. I told Greg and Elizabeth Elliott. They were great friends of mine; I had been friends with Elizabeth, who worked in one of the branches of the newspaper, long before I found out that my indoor cricket batting partner was her husband, Greg! I love them both equally, and I was lucky that they shifted out to New Zealand soon after I did. They obviously understood.

I also told my best friend, Fanie. I first met Fanie through another good friend, Christian. We just clicked. For a while, Fanie and I shared a house with Christian and his husband, Will. Even when I moved out and bought a house and started dating Barbara and we moved in together, Fanie would come over every week on a Thursday for dinner. To this day, every single Thursday night I think about him. It is such a great tradition to have: Thursdays friends come over, have a feed and drink some wine. Fanie still lives in South Africa, but I don't begrudge him his life and he doesn't begrudge me mine, even though I miss him every day and hope he misses me.

Just about everyone I meet asks me why I left South Africa. Simple, really. Allow me to explain.

My best friend Fanie came to visit me in New Zealand in December 2006. He was my rock during my break-up with Barbara.

I've always been blessed with really good neighbours. In my last days in South Africa, I was living in a townhouse that was one of 17 in the same U-shaped complex with a gate at the entrance. We all looked out for one another, and just as well. In the middle of the night not long before I left the country, I got a text from the neighbour living across the way from me. She had got up to go to the bathroom when she heard a strange noise. She happened to glance out of her bedroom window, and lucky for me that she did.

I was woken by my phone with a text from her.

'Someone just climbed into your kitchen window,' it read. 'We are on our way. Arm yourself.'

Well, that woke me up! The three of us — Barbara, the boy and me — were upstairs. I grabbed my cricket bat and ran downstairs into the kitchen. There I found a shadowy figure hidden under a dark hood and wearing blue overalls climbing in the window. He was quite big — around 6 feet — and muscly, and he had bent back the burglar bars to make a gap to climb through, but he must have been slightly dysmorphic, because he had got stuck halfway in. He saw me advancing with my cricket bat, and a look of pure terror came over his face. I gave him an almighty smack on the hand with the bat. He got out of the window pretty damn quick and made a run for it. My neighbour from across the way emerged to give chase. She, too, was waving the South African weapon of choice: a cricket bat. Others came out, too, and soon just about everyone from the entire complex was milling about, trying to work out what the fuck was going on. It was chaos! Three more burglars sprinted out and hid under the cars. I wondered how many more there might be.

Everyone knew it could take anywhere up to 20 minutes before the police arrived. These days, my mother was living in a corner unit in the same complex. She had a larger garden than most, so there was plenty of room for baddies to hide. I ran to her house and went through it with my bat held in the ready position to make sure there was no one there.

Once I was satisfied she was safe, I told her to turn all the lights on and lock herself in.

'I'll be back!' I yelled, and went to sprint off in the direction the burglars had taken.

'Urzy!' Mom called after me. I stopped and turned around. It was like a movie — my mother in her dressing gown, dishevelled from being so rudely awoken, the light from the doorway spilling into the yard, illuminating me, standing there in my jim-jams with my trusty bat in my hands. 'Why do you have a cricket bat?' she asked.

"IT WAS LIKE A MOVIE — MY MOTHER IN HER DRESSING GOWN, DISHEVELLED FROM BEING SO RUDELY AWOKEN, THE LIGHT FROM THE DOORWAY SPILLING INTO THE YARD, ILLUMINATING ME, STANDING THERE IN MY JIM-JAMS WITH MY TRUSTY BAT IN MY HANDS."

'Ma, those bastards were in my house! I have to defend myself,' I said.

'OK.' She nodded. 'I was just wondering why you would run around with a bat when you've got all those guns at your place.'

That was the first time it even crossed my mind. We had a safe containing a couple of handguns that Barbara had inherited. For a fleeting second, I wondered why I hadn't grabbed one. After all, it's what South Africans famously do.

Soon afterwards, the police showed up. They quickly rounded up all four burglars, only to release them again right away, saying they had insufficient evidence to arrest them for a crime. Attention then turned to those who had lately been hitting people with cricket bats, and we all got a telling-off from the police, who took a dim view, they said, of 'out-of-control, vicious vigilantes'.

'Thank God I didn't grab a gun,' I was thinking. If I'd had a gun, in the heat of the moment, I might actually have shot someone. And then, quite apart from the fact that I would have to live with the knowledge that I had actually SHOT SOMEONE, I would probably have been charged with murder — especially since the bent-back burglar bars and broken glass of my kitchen window weren't enough to satisfy the cops that I had been being burgled.

Lots of South Africans have handguns, and I can see why. We had handguns in our house. I have no view about handguns in South Africa, either way: if you have them, you have them; if you don't, you don't. But my first instinct, upon receiving a text telling me that someone was in my house, was to keep myself safe with my cricket bat. Nothing can be read into that except for the fact that I had played indoor cricket the night before. But I am forever grateful that it was my bat and not a gun that I thought of first. Smashing someone on the hand with a cricket bat did not change the course of my life — I'm looking at you, Oscar Pistorius. Having a gun to hand, as so many South Africans do, can turn a dangerous situation so much worse.

To this day I can see the intruder's face when I swung the bat. I can just imagine the horror if I had shot him; the scenario is on constant replay in my head, and I'm glad it's all imaginary rather than a memory to haunt me as I cool my heels in a prison cell.

Another silver lining is that we never had any trouble at that complex again. Some reckoned the police were just lazy: no one got hurt (well, no one innocent), nothing got taken, so why bother with all the paperwork that arresting four perps would involve? Me, I credit the police with a much more subtle psychological approach. I personally believe that word got out amongst the criminal fraternity.

'You see that complex there? Stay away from there, man! It's full of deranged cricketers in onesies.'

In case you're curious, South Africa has comparatively enlightened views when it comes to personal firearms — compared with the US, that is. A significant proportion of the population is armed to the teeth, but the government has made it easy for anyone who wants to disarm to get rid of their weapons. They occasionally extend amnesties, where you can hand in guns and ammunition, no questions asked, and all that evil steel gets melted. That's what happened to the guns that Barbara owned.

Working for a newspaper in South Africa, you were about as close as you could get without working in the police or emergency services to the unnecessary violence and total disregard for life, safety and respect for each other that was increasingly part of daily life. We would get all the police photos of the aftermath of robberies and violent crime. It's like any accident scene: you can't help but look, and then you can't help but remember.

I saw some horrific things. In 2005, the paper ran the story of three 10-year-old boys who gang-raped a 10-year-old girl in a local school. 'When the fuck did this start happening?' I wondered. When I was 10, I was engaged in a titanic struggle not to give in to my urge to eat the yellow crayon. Yet here were kids that same age who were onto sex already. This was on the back of a violent spate of infant rape — actually, I don't think there's any other type of infant rape, is there? Some genius had put about the idea that if you have sex with a virgin it'll cure AIDS. When confronted with the problem of how you can be sure your victim is a virgin, the same genius or others like him decided that you play it safe and have sex with a newborn. Those stories made me very angry, sad and extremely fearful to live in a country where that was not only a thing, but an alarmingly common thing.

How common? An estimated 500,000 rapes take place in South Africa every year and, according to the South African police (if you believe Wikipedia), more than 41 per cent of those are on children and 15 per cent on infants and very young children. It hurts my head and my heart to think about it and I want to lash out and kill every motherfucker who would hurt a child.

I knew that staying there, especially in the actual information circle that distributes the news about that kind of abuse, would make me bitter, angry and twisted. But I can't leave the subject without saying that, while nothing excuses a grown man who rapes a child, I think the government carries a lot of the responsibility for each and every one of these awful crimes. There is not a lot of accurate AIDS education and support. People see so many deaths from or related to AIDS and they panic; they don't know what to do. The government really needs to show some leadership, but fat chance of that. In 2005, the president of South Africa, Jacob Zuma, was charged with raping a lesbian woman, the daughter of a friend of his, in his home. He knew she was HIV positive but he did not use a condom. When asked whether he was worried about contracting the disease, he shrugged and said he had taken a shower afterwards.

His defence against the rape charge was as dodgy as his understanding of prophylactic medicine. The sex was consensual, he said, and when asked how he knew she was consenting, his answer relied heavily on the fact that she was wearing a skirt. Well, we are all in deep trouble, aren't we? When the leadership is as rotten and corrupt as that, there is very little hope.

> **"I KNEW THERE WAS NO WAY I WANTED TO RAISE A CHILD IN THIS COUNTRY, WITH THE CRIME AND THE RAPE AND THE CORRUPTION."**

So you can see what I mean when I say the camel was already reporting severe back trouble when the final straw was dropped on it. One day — Friday the thirteenth, as it happened — four men strolled into the newspaper offices off the street. They had guns. Most businesses in South Africa have very high security — gates, armed guards at the gate, signs promising an armed response . . . if you can think it, they will have it. Because of the line of work we were in, we needed to be accessible to the public, who we encouraged to walk in with stories, photographs and classified advertising copy. We naturally preferred that our visitors weren't armed.

Over the space of five to ten minutes, these four guys circulated through the office, relieving us of wallets, bags, cell phones, car keys (and cars) and even clothes. It was all quite calm. They didn't shout or even really threaten; everyone knew what they were there for, and what it might mean if anyone decided to try to find out if the guns were loaded. Once they'd got everything they wanted, they walked out the way they'd walked in. It was over, but for the rest of the day — and for a few days after that — any unexpected noise would make us all jump, in case they or others had come back to do it again.

'That's it,' I thought. 'I need to get out. I need to get out quickly.'

I knew there was no way I wanted to raise a child in this country, with the crime and the rape and the corruption. The next day, I saw an ad in the paper with a headline that read: 'Want to emigrate?'

'YES,' I thought. 'YES I DO!'

'Why not New Zealand?' the ad asked.

I thought about it.

'You know what?' I told the ad. 'I can't think of a single reason why not.'

Three months after I saw that ad, I was on my way to New Zealand.

The One About THE LAND OF MILK AND HONEY

Leaving was a disaster. My family and a few friends came to the airport to see us off. Barbara's family was there, too, and so was her ex, who was loudly telling anyone who would listen that she didn't want Barbara or the boy to go. She even said she would kidnap the boy, if she had to.

Johannesburg airport was crowded. It was as though whole droves of people were leaving. Barbara was up ahead of me, walking with her family while I walked with mine. But any hopes I had of sharing a final few, precious moments with my mom, my family and my friends were shattered. Suddenly I couldn't see Barbara. She was nowhere to be seen in the crowd waving goodbye to those going through, and nor could

I see her beyond them. I stopped, unsure what to do. Should I go through, in case she was already on the other side? Or should I wait on this side, just in case she was having trouble with her ex? What if her ex had made good on her threats to steal the boy?

I tried phoning her. There was no answer.

In the end, I decided I couldn't risk missing the flight in case she and the boy were on it, but I was still distracted as I said my goodbyes. I went through. Barbara and the boy were at the departure gate. Relief gave way pretty quickly to fury, and we had a ding-dong, stand-up domestic right there and then. We were still bickering when we got on the plane.

As we taxied out and I looked back at the lights of the terminal where my family would be standing, I started crying. I didn't regret anything about my decision to leave South Africa, even now that I was doing it. But I had wanted to help my mom and my friends feel better about it by saying a proper goodbye. I cried for the next two hours, as the plane climbed into the darkness and we left South Africa behind.

It was a long flight. The boy had never flown long-haul before, and was excited by it all — for a while. Like me, Barbara had lived for a while overseas, so we knew the drill. By the time we stopped over in Singapore, we were being civil to one another once again.

We set foot in New Zealand for the first time in my life on Wednesday 21 June, 2006. It was chilly in the cavernous arrivals area at Auckland International Airport, but nothing on what it was outside. It was really fucking cold — bitterly cold, not just the cold that you expect in midwinter in Auckland, which lies more or less on the same latitude as Melbourne. Our adoptive land laid on some extreme weather for our first week: it was supposed to have been the coldest winter for more than 60 years. Funnily enough, the cold made me happy. I didn't have a clear idea of what New Zealand would be like before we travelled, but I was expecting it to be the kind of cold that the Swiss Alps would be in winter. I had visions of everything very white, cold and antiseptic, and imagined that I would live like Heidi: never warm again, but with an elderly man somewhere who would love me, even though he came across as cold and aloof. OK, there was no elderly man, but a girl can dream, and the weather wasn't half as bad as I thought it would be.

"I HAD VISIONS OF EVERYTHING VERY WHITE, COLD AND ANTISEPTIC, AND IMAGINED THAT I WOULD LIVE LIKE HEIDI."

Before we left, we had jacked up a homestay through an emigration agency in South Africa. It was run by a couple of expat South Africans in Torbay on Auckland's North Shore. They were in their fifties and had been living in Auckland for quite a few years. They had put up lots of South Africans on their way to a new life in their time. I'm not sure what they made of us. I think they thought we were just friends, together for convenience's sake while we moved to a different side of the world. But, after a couple of nights, they seemed to suss the fact that we were aliens — or alien to their homophobic little world, anyway. They made it plain that we were no longer welcome in their home, but, credit where it's due, they didn't just leave us in the lurch. They set us up with Chris and Charmaine, good friends of theirs, who were (and are to this day) lovely. They were expats, too, originally from Cape Town, but well settled in Auckland. We stayed with them for three weeks, but even once we moved out I stayed in touch with them and they are part of my family now. They were the only people I had for the first few Christmases and Easters and just when I needed someone in general. Charmaine still pops in for a visit on her way to work at Waitakere Hospital around the corner from my house.

There were lots of other South Africans on the North Shore, but not much fellow feeling. The first guy we stayed with — to protect the innocent, let's call him John — sold me a crappy 1995 Mitsubishi RVR. He asked for top dollar, and his sales pitch failed to mention its many faults and foibles, not least of which was a dodgy gearbox. I trusted him because he was a fellow countryman, a fact that he exploited. Lots of others did the same thing in our early days — not all of our fellow South Africans were shitbags (quite the opposite; I was on the receiving end of some amazing acts of kindness) but, trust me, it hurts all the more when you're fucked over by one of your own.

Newly arrived South Africans are easy to spot, especially by their compatriots, who call them 'kyk-das', for their habit of walking through a supermarket pointing this way and that at the familiar but strange cereals and soft drinks and saying, 'KYK DA! KYK DA!' ('Look there! Look there!' in Afrikaans). We were approached a couple of times in our first week in Auckland by expats who asked us all the expected questions about which part of the Republic we were from, when we'd arrived and so on. All too often — twice in our first week, in fact — our excitement at these encounters was spoiled when we were asked if we had immigrated because we'd had enough of 'the kaffirs' — a racial slur for black people.

'What did you ask me?!' I'd say in disbelief.

'The kaffirs. Too much, eh? Time to get out,' they would reply, with knowing looks. I would then feel obliged to lose it at them, right there in the fruit and veg aisle of the supermarket, pointing out to them that we had a six-year-old and they had (as they did, in both cases) children with them, too, and that they ought not to expose children to hate-speech like this. Let's not raise another generation who feels obliged to fuck up the world because they give a shit about the colour of someone's skin, or sexual orientation, or whether they thought Fords were better than Holdens or Coke better than Pepsi . . .

"LIKE MOST OTHER SAFFAS, WE WERE REFUGEES OF A SORT, SIMPLY DESPERATE TO ESCAPE THE RAMPANT CRIME AND CORRUPTION OF OUR HOMELAND."

I realised quite quickly I couldn't cope living amongst those assholes, because I would almost certainly run into them again. The hunt was on for real to find somewhere else to live. Neither Barbara nor I had bothered with the paperwork necessary to live and work in New Zealand. We came over in the hopes of getting a job, and we were far from alone in that regard. Like most other Saffas (as South Africans get called by New Zealanders, when they're not getting called Japies), we were refugees of a sort, simply desperate to escape the rampant crime and corruption of our homeland. I had sold everything I owned in Benoni, and I figured that we had enough to last us about three months. It would have been stressful for any couple, and for Barbara and I, who were growing less compatible by the day, it was just about intolerable. We were fighting all the time. It was a terrible period in my life and, I'm sure, in hers.

Eventually we found a place in Lynfield way out in

Auckland's western suburbs that the owners were happy to let to us without paperwork. We moved in the same day we answered the ad. Moving our stuff didn't take long. We had nothing except for our bags, a pair of blow-up mattresses that we'd just bought and a blanket each. It all fitted in the boot of our crappy car. As we were unpacking the boot, I saw our elderly neighbours peering into our front door from their upstairs window. I knew they would pop around.

Alva and Barry had lived in their house for many, many years. They had seen hundreds of people come and go from our new (to us) renter.

'You guys all moved in?' Barry, their spokesman, asked.

'Yup,' I replied.

'You don't have much stuff,' Barry observed.

'Nope,' I agreed.

'You'll freeze to death in this house!' Barry protested, and as we stood there in the chill, draughty hall, our breath hanging in clouds around us, I knew he was right. It was colder inside than it was outside, and we soon came to regard this as typical. Like lots of houses in New Zealand, which had been settled by Englishmen who were in denial of its subtropical, maritime climate, it had no insulation and was turned resolutely away from the sun. That didn't matter so much, because it had trees all around it that would have blocked the sun, anyway.

'Oh, well,' I thought. 'We won't have to pay to run a fridge.'

Barry and Alva turned around and went back home, while we got busy not unpacking our tons of stuff. Barry returned about 20 minutes later with a heater, some firewood, cups, plates and quite a few other bits and bobs. Perhaps the most thoughtful gift he brought was cardboard to put under the blow-up mattresses so we wouldn't freeze to death.

*

We had a place, but we still didn't have jobs or even the legal right to expect to have them. I was horribly conscious of our money, how little we had, and how soon we wouldn't have any. I wouldn't buy anything. I had a running argument with Barbara about this: she thought we could afford a plastic rubbish bin to put our rubbish in, but I disagreed. We could get by using plastic shopping bags, and that's what we did. It did my head in that Barbara bought stuff apparently without any thought for our situation.

The bike was just about the final straw. She had promised her boy that she would buy him a bike as soon as we were settled in our new country, so now that we had somewhere to live, she bought him a bike. Of course I hit the roof. I'd had the feeling for a while that we would probably break up, and it now began to seem more like a certainty.

We tirelessly looked for work. A measure of how desperate we were — and how sloppy we were about our research — was that when Barbara got a job interview in New Plymouth, we decided she had to go. I googled New Plymouth and saw that it was only 361 kilometres away — three hours' drive in South African terms. I did the math in my head: three hours there and back, six hours' driving, maybe an hour for the interview and a bite to eat . . . we could easily do it in a day!

So we jumped in our crappy car and headed south, trying to ignore the strange rattles and groans from the mechanicals. A headlight failed somewhere in the Waikato, two hundred kilometres south and halfway to our destination, so we stopped to buy a new one. And it became painfully obvious, as the road got narrower and windier, that I had been wildly optimistic in my time/distance estimates. With the stop for the bulb, it took close to five hours to get to New Plymouth. We were all tired. The boy was the most tired and cranky of all of us, and he had a bit of a meltdown when I took him to the black-sand beach for a walk in the biting wind. The interview took 20 minutes, then we drove for four and a half hours to get back to Auckland. Barbara didn't get the job.

We had enough money for another week, perhaps two, before we would have to get back on the plane and return to South Africa with our tails between our legs and try to beg our old jobs back, when Barbara finally got a job offer. That strengthened my case, as we now had a firm basis on which to apply for work permits, and so I got offered a job in advertising that same afternoon.

The boy was in school and Barbara and I worked, and now we could develop some sort of normal routine. We could even buy stuff — we bought beds and household stuff, and we even bought two little plastic pedal bins to put our rubbish in. Who would have thought that two little plastic rubbish bins could symbolise so much? They were representative of the fact that even I had relaxed my tight fist to the point where we could contemplate this sort of extravagance. I still have them. Also symbolic was when we took the stuff that had kept us alive the first few weeks back to Barry and Alva. Good people: they took the borrowed items back with obvious relief, and you could see that they had been stressing about us down there in the permafrost.

Being officially a suburban Kiwi, I started doing stuff that I'd never dreamed of doing in South Africa, where there isn't so much a do-it-yourself attitude as a get-help culture. In South Africa, there are unemployed people sitting on the side of the road every weekend. All you need to do is stop and ask, 'Who can tile?' Someone will put up their hand, so you take them home, they tile and you give them lunch and pay them a daily wage. Same thing goes with cleaning the house, ironing and so on, and same goes for gardening, too. I can do housework stuff because I never really had a housekeeper (aka 'maid'), but even we had a gardener who would work in our garden once a week.

New Zealand is different. Being so far from the colonial mothership (from anywhere, really, for that matter), they've got used to being self-reliant, so doing stuff themselves — everything from painting a roof or laying a concrete slab to dropping a big Holden V8 engine block into a Toyota Corolla — has become second nature, and something of a badge of honour.

It was a bit of a shock when I learned that we, as tenants, were responsible for keeping the garden tidy. I'd used an electric lawnmower before, but never a petrol-driven one. Still, I liked the idea of getting stuck in! We only had about two square metres of lawn, so no need for a lawnmower. My research indicated that an edge trimmer ought to do the trick. I'd never used an edge trimmer, but I knew they existed and roughly where to get one, so I rocked up to a Bunnings with no more clues than that. I grabbed one off the shelf at random, and one of the staff came up.

'Need any help?' he asked.

'Sure do, pal!' I said, or words to that effect, and by the stupid stuff I started asking, I think he correctly guessed he was dealing with an absolute edge-trimmer virgin. I walked out of the store with everything the most anxiety-prone health and safety expert could have dreamed up, and more. I had gloves, hard hat, safety glasses, boots, ear muffs (and ear plugs, just in case) and mask. I also had the edge trimmer, which was the least significant item on the receipt.

As soon as I was home, I put all the safety gear on, mixed

the two-stroke oil and the petrol, tipped the mix in the edge trimmer and tried to start it.

'Will I have any trouble starting it?' I had asked in the shop.

'Nah, mate. You'll have no worries starting it up,' the salesman had replied.

> **"I WALKED OUT OF THE STORE WITH EVERYTHING THE MOST ANXIETY-PRONE HEALTH AND SAFETY EXPERT COULD HAVE DREAMED UP, AND MORE."**

Well, with all due respect to Nostradamus there in Power Tools at Bunnings, I had a few 'worries'. I pulled and pulled on the recoil starter cord until I had a blood blister on my palm and — now, this is difficult to achieve, especially with all that safety gear on — a rope burn on my face and neck. In fact, I had nothing but fucking 'worries' at this point. The thing was clearly straight out of Satan's fucking tool cupboard.

I decided that Barry might be able to help, so I grabbed the trimmer and ran next door. Barry looked at me, all red and sweaty in my full body armour, frowned at the trimmer, gave the cord a gentle tug and it roared into life, wreathing us both in stinky blue smoke. That was a good thing, because it meant he didn't see how angry, bitter and impressed I was.

No way was I risking the thing cutting out again before I got home. Barry told me I wouldn't have any worries, and carefully showed me how to start it. But I wasn't taking any chances. When he fired it up without difficulty for the third or fourth time, I told him to leave it running. I would have been a sight to behold, and no mistake: a fat foreign woman running down the street in full safety gear, boots and goggles (completely fogged up from the sweat), mask amplifying her ragged breathing like Darth fucking Vader, her slightly over-large hard hat canting at an eccentric angle on her head — and a revving power tool in her hands. Two ladies walking in Lycra screamed and ran away. I did not give a shit! I had two metres of grass that was going to meet its maker before the quarter-litre of fuel in the little plastic tank was gone.

Once home, I set to work.

Edge trimmers look easy to use, but don't let looks deceive you. You'll be delivering a nice, even crew-cut when all of a sudden you'll slightly adjust the plane of that blur of spinning nylon, there will be a violent jerk and a *zut!* noise, your safety goggles will suddenly be spattered with dirt and grass, and there will be a crescent-shaped chunk out of the lawn, which will serve as Exhibit A when someone comes to charge you with being incompetent at trimming grass in a foreign land.

I wasn't defeated! In fact, I was strangely exhilarated as I stepped back to reveal the ruins of my lawn. Oh, I'm much better at it now. I can start my own edge trimmer, lawnmower and the chainsaw that I recently purchased, which is probably a good thing, considering the fuss it would cause if I had to run down a quiet suburban street in full safety gear with a revving chainsaw.

I've painted rooms, I've broken down walls, I've hired a jackhammer and smashed up some concrete — no, no, I know what you're thinking, and I'm not that kind of tenant; this was on my *own* home — and dug up more concrete that covered the yard of the weird section of my home when I bought it and had it removed, all 40 tons of it. Who says we immigrants don't make an effort to fit in?

The One About THE BREAK-UP

Barbara and I had been living in New Zealand for five months and were almost in a domestic routine when I got a call from my mother. My sister was pregnant and she and her English boyfriend were going to get married in a month's time. No one expected me to return to South Africa for the wedding; I'd only been gone a short time, and it's not as though I had left in a private jet. At first, I didn't think I'd go back, either, but after thinking about it for a week I rang my mother and told her that there was just no way that I could NOT go. I swore her to secrecy and bought a ticket.

Barbara wasn't happy about me going at all. In fact, looking back, while I think I had known for a long time that things weren't working between us, it was her reaction to this trip that sealed the deal.

It was a strange feeling, being back on the ground in South Africa. Mom had asked Fanie to go to the airport to pick up some relatives of my soon-to-be brother-in-law, Dave, and his face when he saw me walk out was priceless. We both squealed like schoolgirls! It was so good to see him and all of the other friends I'd left behind only six months before.

It was a great wedding, albeit a little strange. Because my sister had moved away, first to Cape Town and then to the UK, she only had about six of her friends there. The rest of the guests consisted of my mother's friends and colleagues and my friends. But it was great fun! My brother was living in Mozambique because of a rather bad case of drug addiction that he had managed to pick up in South Africa. My sister and her new husband had booked to go and stay with him in a fancy guest house right on the beach for 10 days, but realised too late that Dave's passport wouldn't allow it. My mother and I nobly volunteered to go on their 'honeymoon' instead.

I hadn't previously given Mozambique much thought, but found it to be a beautiful country, if obviously poor. It has only recently emerged from a half century of unrest and violence — the usual African struggle for independence, followed by a nasty civil war (is there another kind?) fomented by, amongst others, the apartheid government in South Africa, which couldn't be doing with a communist neighbour. The conflict broke out in 1976, just two years after the country won its independence from Portugal, and ended only in 1996. It's too much to ask that you'll become a happy-go-lucky, fully functional state after all that: look around you from the air-conditioned comfort of your tourist bus and you'll notice the complete lack of infrastructure and the large number of kids (I counted 10) walking around with automatic weapons. But the house was huge — two storeys, four bedrooms — and right on the beach. It was gorgeous, and hot, and so quiet that in the evening you could sit on the balcony and watch the sea turtles haul out and dig holes to lay their eggs in. Did I mention hot? My brother didn't have any shoes, so I gave him my sandals, only to find out why he wanted shoes so badly. I got blisters on the soles of my feet!

> **"I LOVED BEING BACK IN AFRICA, WATCHING THOSE SUNSETS THAT ONLY AFRICA CAN LAY ON, SPENDING TIME WITH MY MOM AND WITH MY BROTHER."**

You would think there would be lots of resentment amongst the Mozambique locals for the part South Africa played in keeping the civil war raging, but no. With tourism being about the only industry worth speaking of, they know which side their bread's buttered on, and besides, the default setting for Africa and Africans is hospitality. Everyone we met there was just lovely to us. I loved being back in Africa, watching those sunsets that only Africa can lay on, spending time with my mom and with my brother — although the great insight I gained into my brother was that he had a pretty impressive drinking problem. You don't realise when you only see people on holiday that they are out-and-out alcoholics, because everyone sits there and drinks too much and then you return to your normal life and level of alcohol intake. But when you are on holiday and they are leading their normal life and you're still all drinking too much, you realise, 'Uh-oh!' Probably thanks to his unsettled childhood being shifted from pillar to post every time my deadshit dad got pissed and picked a fight with a workmate and had to move on, Quintin has had addiction issues for much of his life. He dabbled in hard drugs and spent some time in rehab. When he got clean from drugs, he started drinking. But he has since cleaned himself up and lives in New Zealand these days. He's a big one for setting himself huge challenges, which he totally dedicates himself to achieving.

*

I flew back to Auckland after 12 days in Africa and landed at midnight. Barbara and the boy had come to pick me up from the airport, and as soon as I saw her I knew our relationship was over. It had run its course. There was nothing in it for us anymore.

There was no great argument to mark the moment it all broke down. Well, there was one around Christmas day. Fanie came out to visit me for six weeks over the Christmas period. He hadn't really got on with Barbara while we all lived in South Africa, and nothing had changed now that we had emigrated, especially not now that both Barbara and I could see the writing was on the wall. Fanie and I came home after a night out to find Barbara had locked us out of the house. That caused a bit of friction, as you might say, but that was really the only bad bust-up. The actual decision that she should move out about a month later was made quite calmly, and without tears or heartbreak on either side. All the same, it could have been quite a shitty time in my life. But Fanie was there, and he was my rock, always ready with a joke and a glass of red wine when I needed one.

Barbara and the boy still live in Auckland, on the North Shore with the rest of the Japies. We still talk to each other and it's all very civilised. We keep a respectful distance from one another, we still give a shit about what happens in one another's lives, but in the end she's my ex and my wife will never be her best friend.

As for the boy, he's taller than me, his feet are way bigger than mine and his voice has broken, so that's a man, right? In spite of the rocky row his mom and I had to hoe, he's a good boy and he's turned out to be a very well-mannered, even-tempered young dude, and I like having contact with him. I won't try to take credit for his calmness: his mother deserves all of that.

The One About ODD JOBS

For the first few weeks in New Zealand, I did a few odd jobs. Well, the jobs weren't odd, but the guys I worked for definitely were. The first offer I got was for a job as a graphic designer, and I immediately started the process of applying for a work permit.

'Can you start straight away?' my prospective boss asked. 'I'll take over the paperwork for you.'

'Er, is it legal, if I don't have a permit?' I asked.

'Sure is!' he said. 'Just think of it as training. You'll hit the ground running when you get your visa!'

So I started. I worked — sorry, 'trained' — for one week, and there was no word on the working visa. Then another week went by. I asked him if I could see the paperwork, and he looked a bit shifty. I picked up my bag and told him he could shove his fucking job — I mean, 'training' — up his ass. This bastard was just using me as slave labour, and I was terrified that word would get out that I had been working illegally and I'd be chucked out of the country. I walked home crying (in the rain, of course), convinced my dream of making a new life as a Kiwi was over.

So far as I know, no one ever found out — until now, I suppose.

Three weeks later I landed a second job — again, as a graphic designer — that was with a very gay guy. 'Yippee!' I thought. 'I'm amongst "family"! This will be heaps better.'

"THIS BASTARD WAS JUST USING ME AS SLAVE LABOUR, AND I WAS TERRIFIED THAT WORD WOULD GET OUT THAT I HAD BEEN WORKING ILLEGALLY AND I'D BE CHUCKED OUT OF THE COUNTRY."

I got a work permit and it looked as though things really were going to be OK. Then I realised there wasn't a lot of actual work to be done at this 'company'. So far as I could tell, I was only there so that my boss could introduce me to his clients as 'his' graphic designer, and tell them that I would be handling all their advertising and so on. They would pay him and he would immediately go on holiday offshore. I'd be left sitting on my own in an empty office with no actual work to do, feeling guilty about drawing the minimum wage to do it.

This went on for six months. I went to South Africa for 12 days for my sister's wedding, and the operation mysteriously didn't grind to a halt. In fact, no one would have noticed any difference. I thought it would be prudent to keep applying for jobs. I finally found one, a real one, at Ogilvy, an advertising agency. I was employed as a Mac Operator, and occasionally I operated a Mac — when I wasn't doing design, typesetting, cheating in Photoshop, making coffee or doing pretty much anything else they wanted done, ASAP. I worked incredibly long hours. We used to say we were going to make a sign and spray-paint 'SWEAT SHOP' on the outside of the building, because we would easily work between 10 and 15 hours a day. It was disgusting. We would have made the sign, too, but we were too busy. But whenever I wanted to feel overwhelmed I'd think about sitting in an office for six months with absolutely nothing to do and I'd smile and think at least my days were moving faster than they had been when I was working for the LGBTQI+ 'family'. I wasn't at all surprised when I saw in the paper not long afterwards that the 'family' guy was arrested for pinching money.

"YOU FIND A WAY OF GETTING ON WELL WITH PEOPLE WHEN YOU'RE SPENDING MORE TIME WITH THEM THAN YOU WOULD IF YOU WERE SHARING A PRISON CELL."

We worked like dogs — do dogs work like that? I suppose Kiwi farm dogs do — but the saving grace of Ogilvy was that we all got on really well. It was necessity, I suppose. You find a way of getting on well with people when you're spending more time with them than you would if you were sharing a prison cell. People don't get this about the advertising industry, just how hard everyone works. We saw so few people from the outside that we developed a special bond, like prison, or boarding school, only with less 'me' time. If you can stick it out, you end up surrounded by mates and you form friendships that don't need to be nurtured; they'll just always be there. If conversation ever flags, you can always talk about the stuff you went through together. I almost feel bad for people who work in banks or toll booths, or even pilots — wherever you only work a certain amount of hours and then have to rest. There is no rest in advertising. But, as we worked in groups around long tables on anything from billboards to mailers, we just had a great time, chatting and laughing and generally keeping each other sane.

The other thing that people don't understand about the advertising industry is why it's there at all. It's simple, really. Someone has to sell the shit you don't know you need or want. None of us was under any illusion that we were saving the world, or ending poverty, or anything very worthwhile at all. The beast we worked for had no soul. But I still see most of those guys. I enjoyed working with them, and while I didn't enjoy the hours, I had nothing else to do, anyway. I was alone in a country where I had no family and no friends as yet. They became my 'people'.

I left Ogilvy after a year. I got offered another job, this time with Y&R NZ, another ad agency that had approached me with better money and I went with the 'growth'. I had no regrets about the first couple of years working weird and wonderful jobs: they gave me a great foundation.

For the whole time I worked at Ogilvy, I sat across the table from a quiet, very attractive and inexplicably single English guy named Leon Fisk. We just 'got' each other. We were always joking around, and he would say to me at least once a week, 'Urz, you have to go do stand-up comedy.'

To which I'd reply, 'Leon, you're out of your fucking mind.'

Leon was put in charge of deciding what to get me as a leaving gift from the team at Ogilvy. He got me a coffeemaker, two cups and a fake contract to go do an open mic night at the Classic Comedy Bar on Queen Street. He made me sign it in front of everyone and it was beautiful. It was peer-group pressure working in slow motion. I hadn't been in the country for very long and because they were my 'people' and I had no one else, and because they wanted to see me do it, I signed the contract and I agreed to go and do the open mic night. To this day I still have the leaving card with the 'contract' in it.

I think I have always been surrounded by laughter. I think back to when I was in school, I'd always be in trouble for talking and making other kids laugh, or for letting fly with my booming laugh that would reverberate around the otherwise very quiet classroom. Teachers were always asking me if I thought I was some kind of clown or a comedian. I didn't think I was, but I

"TEACHERS WERE ALWAYS ASKING ME IF I THOUGHT I WAS SOME KIND OF CLOWN OR A COMEDIAN. I DIDN'T THINK I WAS, BUT I WAS HAPPY THAT THEY THOUGHT I WAS FUNNY."

was happy that they thought I was funny. Throughout the rest of my working life, laughter was a constant. It didn't matter what I was doing or how close to the deadline we were, my workmates and I always found a way to laugh. There's always been a healthy dose of laughter in every office, at every bar and at every drag-race strip where I've ever worked.

But it had never occurred to me that comedy as a profession was an actual thing. I guess I knew there were comedians and comedic actors out there, but I never knew you could just stand on a stage and *that* was your job. I mean, come on. Where do you staple that? How can you put a date stamp on that? And surely the rule was: no date stamp, not a real job. Of course it was a rule! I made the rule, for crying out loud!

Of course, now I know different.

I signed Leon's fake contract on the Friday, woke up with a hangover on the Saturday, remembered, checked the leaving card and the contract, and yup. The open mic was on Monday.

No sweat, assholes. I got this.

Of course, I was very nervous. I can't even begin to tell you the amount of nervous poos I did from the moment I signed the contract to the moment I walked out on stage. When I tell people how terrifying I found the whole thing, they quite reasonably ask why I didn't just pull out after I signed the contract. The answer is simple, really: because I didn't want to look like a dick. I was pretty sure a lot of people were expecting me to pull out and so I didn't want to give them the satisfaction. I had the whole weekend to think about it. I wrote something down, read it aloud with the timer going and thought, 'That's three minutes. Allow two minutes for laughter, and there's your five minutes, right there!'

Oh, what a fool I was, assuming they would laugh. If I know anything about this business after doing over a thousand shows, it's that you can't predict an audience.

The card that Leon gave me when I left Ogilvy, featuring a fake contract to do an open mic night. This was the card that changed it all.

The One About A STAR IS BORN

So I'm walking down Queen Street in the middle of Auckland, just like I've walked down Queen Street lots of times. It's a nice evening — real nice. What they call 'balmy' on the TV weather. It's a Monday. I'm shitting myself.

Nothing about the evening or Queen Street is different. Well, the hundreds of slightly drunk people dressed up in green surrounding me aren't an everyday thing, but it's Saint Patrick's Day, so there's kind of a rational explanation. I'm sweating like anything.

I arrive at my destination. It's an older building, just up the road from Auckland's baroque-ish town hall. It was an adult movie theatre in another life, which would be funny, but I don't want to think about that just now. I take a deep breath and walk in. There are people drinking, sitting at tables in what they call a cabaret-style arrangement. There is a stage, and someone up there is talking into a microphone. Some people are laughing. Some people are not.

Some people are waving at me. They're my workmates. I put on a bright, confident smile and wave back. As I walk over to them, I will everything about my body language to tell them: 'I've got this.'

I so *don't* got this, but there's no way I'm telling them that, and I'm not telling them that I've spent the last two hours since we all saw each other at work sitting in my car, sweating and shitting myself and going over my material again and again.

After meeting and greeting my mates, I walk up to the bar and ask for Chris Brain, who is meant to be the MC for the evening. He's not on tonight. The man who comes out is Steve Wrigley. He introduces me to the bar manager, Nigel Grant, who tells me to call him 'Mash'.

'How are you feeling?' Steve asks.

'Shitting myself,' I say.

Steve laughs.

'You'll be fine,' he says.

I bet he says that to all the wannabes, just before they walk out on stage and crash and burn.

Steve shows me into the green room, which isn't even green. It's a very unrestful shade of maroon. It's not too clean and there's a fair amount of graffiti. It's furnished with crappy chairs that look as though there's a good chance they'd fall apart if anyone sat on them. That makes it sort of a given they'll fall apart if *I* sit on them.

There are other comedians here. We chat a bit. Some of them have done this before. Some of them have done it quite a lot. There are one or two others who are comparative newbies, but none of them are like me, doing their first-ever gig. What strikes me is how cocky some of them are. I wonder whether it's false bravado. Bloody hope it is.

The wait is interminable. One by one, the others in the green room head out onto the stage. I try to ignore the sounds coming from outside that door — there's laughter, but, more ominously, there is sometimes something close to silence. The silence unsettles everyone left in the room.

When it's my turn, the blood is rushing in my ears so loudly it sounds like a waterfall close by. I hope I don't faint. Steve introduces me. I walk into the lights and straight to the microphone in its stand at the front of the stage. I grab the stand in a death grip, and marvel at the fact it doesn't break.

> **" WHEN IT'S MY TURN, THE BLOOD IS RUSHING IN MY EARS SO LOUDLY IT SOUNDS LIKE A WATERFALL CLOSE BY. I HOPE I DON'T FAINT. "**

My mouth is dry, and I have to swallow hard before I open it to try to be sure anything will come out. I sneak a quick look at the tables at the front. There are some people there dressed in green, and without having planned it, without even thinking about it, I start talking to them.

'That's great,' I say. 'Green is my favourite colour, but I can't wear it because I always end up looking like Shrek.'

There is laughter. I look up. I see that the room goes back a surprisingly long way, and it is full of people. For a moment, I can't speak. I'm petrified. No, that's not right. Petrified is what you are when you see a spider on the shower curtain, or half a cockroach in your lunch. I am beyond that. The only word I can find for what I feel is terror.

I stare at them. They stare at me. There's nothing else I can do, so I carry on talking.

'It always makes it awkward when I look like Shrek because then people start looking around for Donkey. The only ass around here is mine.'

There's laughter, and there are a few 'Aww' noises from the people who think self-deprecating humour isn't a team sport.

'It's OK.' I smile reassuringly. 'Don't worry. I don't suffer from low self-esteem. I just realised at a real early age that anorexia was not going to be the disease to take me one day. I don't want to go into too much detail but . . . let's just say that as a child I had to be cut out of a hula hoop, and that day I knew . . . I knew I'd be a whole lot of woman, and I'm OK with that. Sure, I'll never be able to skinny-dip. But, honey, I can chunky-dunk with the best of them.'

The audience is laughing quite a bit at this point. I'm probably aware of it at some subconscious level though, because it turns out that when you're really nervous your hearing is affected. In any case, I've been distracted by my left leg, which is shaking uncontrollably. I can't seem to stop it. I suppose if I'm just going to stand around all that nervous energy has to go somewhere. I'm in 'fight' mode from this clearly dangerous thing that I'm doing, but my heart and my mouth are keeping me on the stage — either that or I'm cold-welded to the mic stand by now.

I become aware of an air of expectancy, or restlessness, and I realise with a jolt that I've been quiet for too long.

'I'm South African,' I say. 'A lot of people have asked me, "Why did you move to New Zealand?" And I say it's simple. Because I'm racist! I hate white people. They can't dance or jump — it's just not right. It's creepy, quite frankly.'

Then I say something about being a 'lesbyterian' and that I know it's disappointing when all the hot ones turn out to be gay but what are you going to do?

I talk a bit more, and somehow I've got to the end of my five minutes. I deliver the closing line — the same closing line that I'll use for about a year after today: 'I want to go now, but before I leave I want to leave you with a little somethin' somethin''. Gay people: stay out, stay proud. Straight people: you taste like chicken.'

I don't know what's going on, then. I'm flooded with relief, and I don't even stop to gauge the level of noise, to work out whether they loved me or . . . not. I'm just so pleased it's over. I'm out of there.

You'll sometimes hear stories about people who do something new like stand-up comedy for the first time and they walk off stage thinking, 'This is it! This is what I'm supposed to be doing with my life!'

That wasn't me.

After that first gig at the Classic, I walked off with a sense of relief that could only be equalled by staying in the desert for three days with no water and then stumbling upon a water truck with cool — but not too cold — water in it and just plunging your face in it. I was sweaty and I was nearly drunk, but I sure as shit didn't have any sort of epiphany. What I had was a thirst. I needed a beer and a sit-down.

The Classic hasn't changed one bit today from how it was on my first ever gig on Saint Patrick's Day in 2008. I rejoined Leon and most of the rest of the agency, who were all packed into the front bar. Leon looked like the cat that got the cream, because it was his suspicion that I could make a go of stand-up that saw me get myself into this crazy mess from the outset. Everyone else was telling me how they didn't think I would go through with it.

'I'd never pussy out of anything!' I protested, not letting on one bit about how close I had been to pussying out. 'If you don't think I can take a dare, you clearly don't know me at all!'

I was lying my tits off, of course. Dares are for dumbasses, and I wouldn't hesitate to back out of anything I didn't feel like doing. Who knows why I didn't pussy out? I think, maybe, part of me really wanted to give it a go. Maybe I was given a boost by Leon's faith in me, and maybe it's because I could see how much poor, shy Leon would love to do stand-up but has never managed to summon up the courage. Maybe it's just because my attitude has always been that if an opportunity presents itself take it, because, well, 'there's no greater waste of time than regret', right?

I was sitting on my third beer after the gig when a bald guy shouldered his way through all the agency types around me and introduced himself as Brendhan Lovegrove. He told me he had watched the show and he had some questions. Who was I? Where did I come from? How long had I been in New Zealand? Did I do comedy in South Africa? How many gigs had I done? Why was I there at the Classic? Why did I do a Monday night?

I said to him, I'm from South Africa, I'd been in the country just a year or so and I'd never done comedy before. This was my first time.

'First time?!' he said. 'Are you fucking kidding me?'

I shrugged and said that I was not.

Brendhan got really enthusiastic. He told me that I had

to carry on with comedy, that he could sense I'd be a good comedian, and I had to come back the following Monday night. At one point, I turned to Leon and said, 'This guy is clearly drunk. I'm no comedian!'

Leon and Brendhan laughed.

'Sure, he's drunk,' Leon said. 'But he's also right.'

Leon joined Brendhan in trying to persuade me that I had to come back and do it again. I just laughed at them, but Brendhan made me promise before he left that I'd come back and that I would have a serious go at doing comedy. I promised. I didn't really care that I would break the promise, because he was just a guy who I'd never see again. As I've said, I'm quite happy pulling out of stuff I don't want to do.

Trouble was, I got home late that night and was buzzing so hard after the gig that I couldn't sleep for ages. I realised I had loved it! I had loved the adrenaline rush and the walking-on-air sensation afterwards. I had only dimly heard the laughter from the crowd — it sounded like it was at a distance and through fog — but the sound kept coming back to me. It was like a drug and I knew I had to get me some more.

I would have loved to talk about it all with someone, but when I got to work the next day, it was my first day in my new job. I didn't know anyone at Y&R, but I told the girl sitting next to me all about it. She seemed interested for a while. I tried to concentrate on my job.

At about 11 am I got the call that changed my life.

'Urzila? It's Mash here, from the Classic.'

'Oh shit,' I thought. 'What did I leave behind?'

'I'm just calling to say congratulations,' Mash said. 'You are through to the next round.'

'What?' I asked.

'The next round.'

'The next round of . . . what?'

'Raw Quest.'

'Raw Quest? What's that?'

'That's where they look for new talent during the comedy festival. We hold competitions and narrow it down to a few each round and you've made it to the semi-final.'

'Oh, no thanks. I just did it as a work thing, a dare, you know. Give it to someone else. I don't do comedy.'

'No,' Mash pleaded. 'You have to do it! You were very funny! Everyone was laughing.'

'Oh, that. Yes, everyone was laughing because I knew seventy people in the audience. We all work together. That's why they laughed.'

'I was in the audience. I laughed. I don't know you.'

That was food for thought.

'Come back and do it again. Don't tell anyone and you can see how it goes.'

I didn't have to think very long or hard.

'OK,' I said.

I ended up doing just that. I went back and I did the semi-final. I wrote a whole new five minutes, because I thought that's how it worked. I thought every time you walked out on stage, you had to do new material.

When I looked out at the audience, I didn't see any familiar faces. I hadn't told a soul I was going to do it, not even Leon. People still laughed. Weirdly, someone recorded it and put it on YouTube, so my second ever gig is on YouTube, if you can be bothered to go look it up. They filmed it in landscape so it's on YouTube sideways, but even if you're tipping your head sideways to watch it, you can see how nervous I was. You can see me swinging from side to side and still trying to hold onto that mic stand with all my might. I know my mouth is really dry and I can see I'm swallowing a lot.

My material (which is what we comedians call our gags) was a lot more lesbian this time around. It was also about shopping and driving. When I watch the clip now, I'm not at the point where I cringe, but I can see how I could make that material better today. It might be my imagination or it might not, but in my second performance I don't look quite so much like a possum in the headlights. I am definitely studying the audience to see how the material is going down.

I finished with the same sense of relief I had first time around, but this time I was open to the thought that I might do it all again. I got a call the next day to say that I was in the Raw Quest finals.

TAKE MY WIFE — PLEASE!

My first appearance as a stand-up comedian was one life-changing event that happened around this time. Another was when I went to watch a rugby game. I had been apart from Barbara for a while now, and I wasn't looking for anyone (so often the way, isn't it?). My great friends Elizabeth and Greg Elliott, who had recently shifted out from South Africa, were heading into town to a bar to meet up with friends to watch the All Blacks play Ireland. I wanted to go into town, too, as I was meeting some friends of mine in a gay bar later on. Elizabeth offered to give me a ride to the bar, so long as I didn't mind watching the rugby first and having a bite to eat while we caught up and she satisfied herself that I was OK after my break-up and not completely running off the rails.

Of course I didn't mind. I love rugby, as I love all sports, and it was as good an excuse as any other to spend time with the Elliotts.

As soon as we walked into the place just off Auckland's Aotea Square, I saw a woman leaning on the bar and talking on her phone.

'I hope the lesbian at the bar is one of the girls you're having dinner with,' I said, you know, joking.

'Don't be stupid,' Elizabeth said. 'Not everyone you fancy is gay!'

Then we walked up to the bar, the woman ended her phone call, smiled at Greg and Elizabeth and turned her big blue eyes on me. She held out a hand to me as Elizabeth did the introductions.

'Urzila, Julie. Julie, Urzila.'

Elizabeth worked at Diagnostic Medlabs — the outfit that does medical analysis for New Zealand's public health system — with Julie and Julie's flatmate. They were phlebotomists (which is people who stick needles in you to get blood out for laboratory analysis). It turns out Elizabeth suspected Julie may have been a lesbyterian but was too shy to ask. She thought the best way to proceed was to introduce us and see what happened.

Well, what happened is that Julie's flatmate took against me, right away. She straight out hated me, and I'm quite sure it's because it was plain to everyone there that the other thing happening that night was that Julie and I were hitting it off. She was just so open and friendly and we clicked.

Julie was officially 'straight' at that point, but her attitude was the same as mine before I came out: there were just people in the world, and what mattered when you were deciding to hang out with someone was the person, not their gender. After dinner, and before I went off to meet my friends at the bar, Julie and I had agreed to see each other again. The date was 7 June 2008. I don't remember it because the All Blacks turned on a particularly memorable performance. I couldn't even tell you if they scored that evening. But when I left the bar, I had a funny feeling I might have.

One of the ironies of the whole situation is that it was common knowledge that I have shit taste in women: I must have inherited it from my mother, only for women instead of . . . you know what I mean. But anyway. Elizabeth had always said that she would be in charge of choosing my wife. In a roundabout way, she was.

A month later, Julie and I officially became an item. This involved Julie coming out. She did it much the same way as I did, with no big issues emerging for anyone and no real surprises. Well, perhaps only one. I thought maybe Julie should tread carefully around her nan, Phyllis, who is in her eighties, and perhaps not tell her, because the older generation don't always take that sort of news too well. Julie and her nan are very close, and I didn't want to be the person responsible for a rift between them. But Julie's attitude was all for one, one for all! If she was telling her family, she was telling her *whole* family. As it turned out, she was a better judge of her nan than me. Phyllis's response blew me away. She was totally cool with it, and she was and is to this day very supportive of our little family. She might have grown up in a world where women didn't marry women, have children and live happily ever after, but she's one of those people who sees through to the important stuff. As long as people are happy and children are happy and well looked after, who cares what the arrangements around them are? That's how it should be.

The best you can hope for is to find someone who you can laugh with and who keeps you in check, to make sure you don't act like a complete dick and blame it on your

> **"AS LONG AS PEOPLE ARE HAPPY AND CHILDREN ARE HAPPY AND WELL LOOKED AFTER, WHO CARES WHAT THE ARRANGEMENTS AROUND THEM ARE? THAT'S HOW IT SHOULD BE."**

environment or circumstances or what-the-hell-ever else. I'm lucky I found a girl who has the same set of values as I have and who has a lot of common interests. Interests, mind, not tastes. We hate each other's taste in music and movies, but when it comes to how to treat people and how we like to be treated and how we want to raise our kids, we are on the same page and that's what's important.

The One About STARTING OUT IN COMEDY

The Raw Quest finals were held at the Classic in May. An Australian comic, Mickey D, was the MC, and there were nine of us competing. I wrote a whole new set for the occasion. With the benefit of hindsight, if I'd done it with older gear, I probably would have acquitted myself better. I was nervous as hell, but it seemed to go OK. I didn't win — that honour went to Cameron 'Pinchy' Murray — but I was named the New Zealand Comedy Guild's Best Newcomer, and also awarded the Andrew Kovasevic Cup for the Most Offensive Gag. For the record, this is it:

My ex and I broke up because she wanted to take our relationship to the next level and I said, sure, let's make it abusive and she didn't like that so we broke up. But then she wanted to get back together again and I said I'd rather be fist-fucked by a leper than take you back.

Missing out on the grand prize didn't bother me, but what it did do was give me a real appetite to keep trying. I knew I could do a whole lot better, and I became determined to try.

"COMEDY IS A SMALL INDUSTRY, AND MOSTLY EVERYONE LOOKS OUT FOR AND SUPPORTS ONE ANOTHER."

Right from the first moment I walked into the Classic that Saint Patrick's Day, people were very supportive. Comedy is a small industry, and mostly everyone looks out for and supports one another. Nothing much changed when I scored my early successes in the Raw Quest. Looking back, I can see that there were one or two who had their claws out: it was a competition, after all, and not everyone takes my attitude — that you just play your own game and let people get on with theirs.

Winning the award gave me confidence. I started doing regular gigs, and I used much of the same material I'd used in my first gig — the opening and closing lines, about being a South African racist, and straight people tasting like chicken. I was happy if my sets were book-ended by laughs. I think the way I had struck out in my first gig was the way I continued: my on-stage persona is just me, but with sweaty palms, having a chat with a lot of people without giving them the opportunity to join in my conversation. My humour has been described as self-deprecating, and that's probably true: the butt of my humour is often my own butt, and I get plenty of mileage out of my nationality (especially the accent) and the fact that I am a lesbian. The laughs all came quite easily at first.

But I began noticing that audiences stopped laughing in the places I expected them to laugh. Then I noticed they stopped laughing anywhere much at all. I was confused. Other audiences had laughed at these jokes; what had gone wrong? Knowing what I know now, it was probably that my delivery was a bit flat. When they didn't laugh, or their laughter was half-hearted, I got scared. And, when the audience senses you're scared, they don't feel safe and secure that they are in the hands of a professional. If you're not confident, then they don't feel confident, and the thrill is basically gone.

"MY HUMOUR HAS BEEN DESCRIBED AS SELF-DEPRECATING, AND THAT'S PROBABLY TRUE: THE BUTT OF MY HUMOUR IS OFTEN MY OWN BUTT."

This 'finding my feet' phase of my career — OK, I sucked — lasted just under a year, and then I began to realise that you need to have confidence in your 'material'. If you radiate confidence, you can take them on whatever journey you want to.

Even after a year I knew that I knew very little about the industry. It's unlike pretty much any other job where you start and there is a manual on how the job goes, or you can set an end result to be achieved. You don't sit down with your manager and do a performance review, and there's no industry training. You have to find your own way through a dark maze.

*

I didn't even know about comedy festivals, which are probably the closest thing comedians have to a gravy train. I heard some comedians talking about Adelaide Fringe and I thought I should have a go at that. In 2009, after less than a year on the circuit, in which time I'd have done about 10 gigs, I packed my bags for a full run at the Adelaide Fringe. I had very little money. By 'very little money', I mean basically zero. I'd never even been to Australia before so I had no idea what to expect. I couldn't afford a hotel or even a sleazy backpackers. A friend offered to share a place with me for $80 per night, but that was too steep, so I found a 'flatmate' for the month on Craigslist.

Craigslist isn't as big in Australia and New Zealand as it is elsewhere in the world. It's an open forum in which people make all kinds of connections — from second-hand goods to ride-sharing to accommodation to casual sex to illegal stuff and, in some notorious instances, it's where serial killers find their victims (hence the modern term 'Craigslist Killers'). I had no choice. I found an ad someone had posted for a flatmate for $150 a week. I googled her to make sure that if it came to fighting for my life I'd have the edge in hand-to-hand combat. She seemed to be a personal trainer and a teacher and apart from being really fit, otherwise pretty normal. I was satisfied. I grabbed the opportunity. Her name was Adrian — still is, actually, which is not universally true of people who advertise on Craigslist — and she turned out to be lovely. We are Facebook friends to this day.

Naturally, I got the crummiest flight I could find, which took about 900 hours to get from Auckland to Adelaide via Sydney, not counting the time-zone thing. It was 2 pm

Australian time when I arrived in Adelaide and it was hot. In fact, in the whole time I was there, I swear the temperature didn't drop below 40 degrees Celsius. My bleary eyes fell gratefully on a coffee cart in the airport. I was tired and I needed a coffee. I assumed a coffee cart would sell me one, and I was encouraged in this belief by the words 'Coffee Caravan' painted on the side. I walked up to the caravan, locked eyes with the girl inside it and, with a tired smile, said, 'How you doing?'

'What do you want?' she replied sourly.

'Coffee,' I replied, as surprised by her rudeness as I was by the question. 'It's all you sell, isn't it?'

She rolled her eyes.

'What *kind* of coffee?'

Maybe I was just used to the friendliness of Kiwis. Maybe I was just pissed off at how short she was.

'Fuck your coffee,' I said, and walked away. I've since come to realise that Australians aren't as ridiculously friendly to foreigners as New Zealanders are. I hope that's because they're too busy for chit-chat at work: What do you want? Place your order and move on. I've met enough extremely friendly Aussies by now to know that the national asshole per capita rate is probably no higher than that of any other country you could care to name.

Despite the heat, my flatmate Adrian ran to work each morning, until I pointed out that she was out of her mind.

'It's too hot,' I said. 'You'll drop dead!'

She must have taken my advice, because the next morning, she was pumping up the tyres on her bike.

I don't think I've ever been that hot in my entire life, and I grew up in Africa! I would freeze water in a plastic bottle so that it was just a solid block of ice. I would put it in my rental car and drive into the city (10 minutes away) and it would be tepid by the time I got there.

I was in Adelaide for five weeks. Adelaide Fringe is the second-largest arts festival in the world and the largest one in the Southern Hemisphere. Along with Justine Smith, a friend I had made on the circuit back home, I got picked up by a promoter — a woman I won't name, because I'll never work with her again — and did her line-up show for a month. I also did every other show I could possibly fit in. There was sort of a snowball effect — if you can have a snowball effect in that heat — where I picked up more gigs on the strength of each one I did. During the 24 nights that I performed, I appeared in nearly 50 shows, just doing five minutes here and there. On some nights I'd do up to five shows. It was hard work and I'd finish exhausted, but I loved it. I relished the opportunity to have that amount of stage time. I met so many people who I still work with today and who I look up to as amazing artists.

"ON SOME NIGHTS I'D DO UP TO FIVE SHOWS. IT WAS HARD WORK AND I'D FINISH EXHAUSTED, BUT I LOVED IT."

It was a difficult time away from home for me, away from Julie, about a year into our relationship. Having Justine there made the trip so much better than it might have been. She had weird accommodation, too, that the nameless promoter had jacked up with one of her friends. Justine and I both craved privacy at home and just to have some time to ourselves, so we spent a lot of time together during the day, exploring South Australia, and at night we'd do our shows and go to see as many other shows as we could and then hang out in the artist bar till closing time. It would be the early hours of the morning when we headed back to our respective homes. We had a ball uniting against the weirdness we faced. We met other comics together who would become friends — Francesca Martinez and Jen Brister from the UK and Aussies Jenny Wynter, Hannah Gadsby, Kerry Reid (aka Miss Patsy DeCline), Geraldine Quinn, Lori Bell and Amelia Jane Hunter, to name a few: there were so many! I also met some promoters who played large roles in my comedy career when I started going to other festivals.

Julie came to visit me for a week. It was great. We explored Adelaide together, and I decided I really liked Australia, the surly woman in the airport coffee caravan notwithstanding. I came, in time, to forgive even her. I figured I'd be cranky too if I was stuck in a caravan all day and all night.

The One About WAXING LYRICAL

People find the whole business of comedy fascinating — rightly so — and one of the things I am most commonly asked is where I get my ideas from. 'Well,' I usually reply, 'just about everything I say on stage is true, to a point.'

Take the example of the Great Adelaide Intimate Waxing Disaster. This is how I tell it on stage:

I was doing the Adelaide Fringe one February. It was steaming hot. They had a heatwave for two weeks where the temperature never dropped below 40 degrees and it was so hot you couldn't actually breathe with your mouth closed. Of course, it's February, so there's a Valentine's Day in there somewhere and I've got a girlfriend — who is now my wife — coming from New Zealand to visit me for a week for Valentine's and my birthday, which is the next day. But, because I've been away from home on tour for about three months at this point, I've let the winter garden grow wild, if you know what I mean [I wave my hand vaguely around my crotch area]. The entertainment area had not been trimmed in a while and the edges are growing over the footpath, so I thought, 'I better get my garden tidy before my girlfriend shows up.' So I looked up a few places to see who has a 'waxologist' I could consult for the big job, and I don't really like going to someone new, because a waxologist is a very close relationship; you have to trust her more than a friend and you grow to love her like a sister, because a good waxologist sees some ugly shit and you want to be sure that as soon as you walk out of that cubicle they won't say a word about what happened in there! You should have the same kind of confidentiality you find between a priest and a parishioner or a doctor and a patient — that type of confidentiality. Alas, you don't always get that, because I've got friends who are beauticians and they tell me some of the horror stories they have witnessed so I know it's not all private!

So, when I met this lady, she seemed lovely and we hit it off immediately. I booked a session — a full one — for the next day. I walked in and her studio was very warm. Like, very warm! I vaguely remember saying something to the effect, 'Holy fuckballs! It's hotter than an armpit in here!' And she informed me that the air-conditioner wasn't working and I still thought, 'Poor bitch.' At least I didn't have to stay long and I won't have pants on so I'll be OK.

I was lying on a little bed and she proceeded to apply hot wax to my nether regions. Now, to those of you who aren't familiar with how waxing works, they apply hot wax to you, then the wax sets, then they rip the wax off, which in turn rips the hair out. You pass out for a few minutes and when you regain consciousness your garden is tidy and you pay your money and you leave. The key, though, is in the wax SETTING!

[The smart ones in the audience begin to chuckle, because they have seen where this might be going.]

Now, on this day, because it was so super hot and the AC wasn't working and I'm a big unit, she applied the wax, but it wouldn't set because it was so hot! All I heard from down below was the last thing you want to hear from your waxologist. She said, 'Uh-oh.'

I calmly asked, 'WHAT?' [I shout this.]

She said, 'It's not setting.'

I could feel the hot wax running into spots that I didn't really want waxed — I didn't want the full possum hairless — but I had a wax butt plug at this point. The waxologist grabbed a piece of cardboard and started fanning the situation, trying to get it to set. I looked down and there she was; it looked like I was giving birth to a little Asian lady. She tried her very best but nothing worked and, of course, the more I stressed about it setting, it definitely didn't want to set because I was just running hotter and hotter, making it impossible to set. She tried for a few minutes, when I checked my watch and told her that I had to leave. She started to panic. She said, 'You can't! We have a Situation!'

I knew I had no option, because I had to go do a show and the people — all nine of them — would not give a shit about my Situation. I had to go do the show, so I did what any woman in my position who has shit to do would have done: I swung off that bed and pulled on my knickers right over the soft wax . . . I tell you what, it felt nice! You can't judge me! Unless you've been there, unless you've had warm, soft wax in your underwear and felt the soft (dis)comfort you have no place to judge me.

I left and I did my show and I had a few beers after the show with my audience. It was a good night, so good that I started to forget about my Situation. I went to the bathroom after a few hours with a 'beer piss'. Now, if you've ever had a beer piss, you'll know that it's far more aggressive than a wine piss. A wine piss will allow you to stop mid-stream if you hear a noise outside the bathroom, while a beer piss will not allow any of that shit. It will go right through the side of the toilet if you don't adjust stream. It's strong and it's wilful! So I ran to the toilet and — completely forgetting about the ball of wax in my pants — whipped off my knickers — and waxed myself! Not in a good way: clumps of skin and wax separated from my body, I blacked out and fell in between the toilet and the wall.

I'm not sure how long I was unconscious for, but when I came to I still needed to pee, so I picked myself up and got on the toilet and started to pee, but nothing came out. [I allow a pause]. My lips were sealed!! I couldn't turn the pee off, though, and it kept coming out and building up pressure in the process and eventually it found the weak spot right at the top and it burst through the wax and a stream blasted me in the face. I had nowhere to go and nothing to do. I just sat there peeing while the pee was blasting me in the face and all I could think was, 'I remember reading somewhere it's good for your skin.'

*

Now when you listen to that, you can either conclude that that really happened to me, or (like most people) you can decide it's too far-fetched.

Here is what actually happened.

I was out with an acquaintance for a drink and he told me, 'You'll never believe what happened to my mother the other day. She went for a wax and the wax wouldn't set because the air conditioning wasn't working. Who doesn't get their AC serviced?!'

That was it! That was his story, and he was appalled by the fact that the air-con equipment wasn't working. But my mind had already raced on ahead. I told him, 'I'm taking that story and I'm making it mine.' Which I did.

OK, so I exaggerated a little bit here and there. But it's something that totally COULD happen to me. I can picture it happening to me. So it's a true story, as far as I'm concerned.

The One About THE MOUSE

Sometimes you don't have to exaggerate the stuff that happens to you (or to me, anyway) to get a good gag going.

Kerry Reid (who goes under the stage name of Miss Patsy DeCline) invited Justine and me to her house for lunch towards the end of our run in that first year we attended the Adelaide Fringe. Justine and I were talking about our accommodation and Kerry said to me that if I ever came back to Adelaide, I should go and stay with her. So in February 2010, that's what I did. She lives up in the Adelaide Hills with her (then) two cats — one has since sadly passed away after a dog ripped him up — and loads of birds and all the assorted snakes and big spiders that you imagine would live in the hills in Adelaide.

I was staying with Kerry and looking after her birds and

cats whenever she went off to work with Clown Doctors in Adelaide. On one occasion, she left for a couple of days to go wherever they were needed. When she came back, she was knackered and, quite frankly, so was I. I had spent most of the time awake because for some reason I thought that all those snakes and spiders were just biding their time until she was out of the picture, whereupon they would swarm or slither or whatever out to get to me. Plus I couldn't find one of the cats. I told myself I wasn't too worried, because he had always come home before. But the night Kerry got back, I was lying in bed, unable to sleep because I was trying not to be worried about the cat. I was reading my book when I heard him come in. I was relieved. I propped myself up on one arm on the bed and looked at him as he lazily strolled into my bedroom.

> **"SO NATURALLY I REACTED AS AFRICAN LADIES WILL WHEN CONFRONTED BY A MOUSE. I SCREAMED AS LOUD AS I COULD!"**

'Where have you been, mister?' I asked.

He just looked at me with that dismissive look that cats give you, then he put something down and meowed at me, as if to say, 'What's it to you, lady?'

I smiled at him, and then in the same moment that I thought to wonder what he had dropped, I realised it was a mouse, and it was very much alive.

Now I'm from Africa, home of some of the larger animals ever to terrorise humankind — elephants, hippos, crocodiles, rhinos, a range of big cats. So naturally I reacted as African ladies will when confronted by a mouse. I screamed as loud as I could!

Kerry came flying into my room. I was standing in the middle of the room with eyes bigger than the palms of my hands.

'Kerry,' I quavered, pointing, horror-struck. 'That cat just dropped a live mouse in this room and I CANNOT —WILL NOT — sleep until I know where exactly it is!'

We started looking for the little baby mouse. We literally flipped everything in that room over and we just could not find it. Eventually — around 3 am — Kerry said, 'I think that mouse is out of the house. It's probably down the road and still going.'

I agreed. We had turned everything upside down, and there had been no sign of it. It must be gone.

She went back to bed, I climbed into my own bed and all the while the asshole cat just sat at the door licking his paw, looking at me with that 'Well, well' look that only cats can wear — you know, the one that says, plain as day, they do not give a flying shit about you or your amusing phobias.

I was too pumped with my brush with death, or whatever it was that I was afraid the mouse would do to me to sleep, so I picked up my book again.

I hadn't read a page before I became aware of a noise, a very quiet but distinct noise, a kind of *tup tup tup tup*.

'Hmm,' I thought. 'That sounds like . . . like . . . a small rodent cleaning its little face!' But if it was a small rodent cleaning its face, I wouldn't be able to hear it unless it was . . . really close to *my* face . . .

I rolled my head to the side and the little mouse sitting on my pillow a few centimetres from my face paused in his ablutions and made eye contact, as if to say that he, too, was glad that whatever had terrified me had now gone and that the cat seemed to have lost interest in him.

I screamed right in his tiny face and jumped out of bed so fast he didn't even move. (Note I'm saying 'he', but I have no clue as to the gender of said mouse. I'm just thinking a girl mouse would have had the sense to think, 'Well, I've already given her an almighty fright tonight. I'll just go find a pillow and have a lie-down in the lounge.' But not this mouse, so I'm going boy mouse.)

Kerry came running back into the room and I pointed to the mouse. She said to keep an eye on him while she went to get a tupperware container. She runs back in with it and hands me the lid. The plan, she explains, is that she will place the container over the mouse and all I have to do is slide the lid in underneath.

In my guestimation, I already know I've been set up to fail. Every time I've ever tried to put the lid on a tupperware container, the theme to *The Benny Hill Show* has started up in my mind. Push down this corner, and that corner pops up. Push down both corners and the other side pops up . . . you know the routine.

"I RAN SO FAST AND SO HARD THAT I DIDN'T ACTUALLY MOVE: I JUST RAN ON THE ONE SPOT FOR A FEW SECONDS TRYING TO CLIMB MYSELF."

Anyway. To cut a long story short, and also because I don't know how to adequately describe the terror and whimpering that came out of me — I'm not proud of it — she had him in the container, I tried to put the lid on but I panicked, or she moved (we are still at odds over what exactly happened) and the mouse must have decided, 'Look. Clearly I'm not welcome. I'll just leave.' He ran out of the container and up my arm. I started running around, trying — I swear — to get away from my own arm. I ran so fast and so hard that I didn't actually move: I just ran on the one spot for a few seconds trying to climb myself. In the process, I managed to stomp on my left foot with my right foot. The mouse was gone, but I was in pain and in shock. Kerry got an ice pack and I looked for a place where I could bury my face and hide from the ignominy of it all. I felt shame — ashamed that a little boy mouse could make me so scared that I could inflict such an injury on myself.

For the remainder of the trip, I was unable to place my full weight on my foot. It was still blue two weeks later when I hobbled home, because I was too embarrassed to go to the doctors in Adelaide. When I finally summoned the courage to consult a doctor back home, a broken bone was diagnosed.

'You were attacked,' I tell myself. 'It wasn't your fault.' But it is a shame I have never quite lived down — largely thanks to Miss Patsy DeCline.

The One About DOING ANAL

That year — the Year of the Mouse, 2011 — was a momentous one, as it was the year in which I dedicated myself full-time to the art of comedy. I had already decided I was ready to leave advertising the following January, when I was providentially made redundant in November 2011. When I walked out of Y&R for the last time, I kissed goodbye to advertising. This was big. Advertising had been a big thing in my life, but I was ready to let it go. I started looking for something else to fit around my comedy commitments. I replied to an ad in the paper looking for a night manager at the Pelican Club in downtown Auckland, which calls itself a gentleman's club but which — get this — is really a brothel! I applied for the position — in light of what followed, I use that term advisedly — because I thought the experience would give rise to an amazingly funny story or two to tell on stage. I got an interview, and I suppose it's natural enough, given the business model, that it was at night. I rocked up and they put me in a room with a few other girls who were all applying for different roles. On stage, I'd say 'positions', but since this is serious literature I'll say 'roles'. Just being in that room was a fascinating experience.

The room was at once very clean and quite dire. I was impressed by the hygiene and a little grossed out at how blatant it was. The only place I could sit was on the bed. Besides the bed, there was a shower, a chair, a little table on which were laid out lube, condoms and tissues. The whole room was covered in mirrors and I remember thinking, 'I don't think I need to see anyone's bits from so many angles in such good lighting!'

I'm not sure what I expected but it was literally just like being in a waiting room for any other job interview. Some of the women who were there were just following the family career line. One was applying to the Pelican because her mother and sister were already working at another similar establishment and she didn't want to mix family and work — just like any other job, I thought.

Some of the women were very young and some were older than me. That struck me: none were just in their mid-twenties to thirties. It was young women starting out and it was women going through divorce or getting back into the workforce after they'd had their kids and who were back to what they used to do. One of the girls had worked there for years and was reapplying after taking a couple of years off to have a baby. One of the newbies asked — professional curiosity, I suppose — what a girl did to fill in all the time she had to spend in there with her client.

'Oh, just let him shower and try to keep him in there for as long as you can,' the old hand said. 'Then get him out and dry him off slowly. By the time it gets down to the business side of things, there's only a few seconds of actual work and then it's all over and done with.'

It was a solid plan, but I was secretly wondering how much Viagra and other magic pills could mess with it.

There wasn't much comedy to be mined out of there. I'm sure if I had accepted the job I would have picked up some jokes, but not because of the industry — more in the lunch room. Those women were amazing! Warrior women! Looking back now, I can't believe that I actually went in there thinking that this would be great research. The funniest thing that happened was one of the ladies asked me if I did anal.

> **"SHE WINKED AT ME. THEY WERE ALL NODDING AND SAYING, 'OH, YES. NIGHT MANAGER,' AND WINKING AND SMILING."**

'No,' I said.

She looked a bit taken aback and a bit concerned.

'Well if you don't do anal, love, you're out of here!' she said. 'These guys don't come in here because they want to fuck you like they can fuck their wives. They want something different! If you don't do anal, well . . . you're fucked!'

I smiled, and said, 'Oh, I'm applying for the night manager's role.'

The other nine women sitting in the room with me just looked at me and smiled knowingly.

'Oh, OK,' the lead one, who had asked about anal, said with heavy irony. 'Sure, doll. So are we!'

She winked at me. They were all nodding and saying, 'Oh, yes. Night manager,' and winking and smiling.

How could I tell them I truly was there just for the night manager role, I wondered. They thought I was making it up. Then I started to worry. 'What exactly does the night manager role entail?' I wondered. I couldn't remember anything about anal in the ad.

In the end, I didn't get the night manager's job. I signed up with a comedy manager instead. Hilary Coe runs Creeping Charlie Productions. We were lone wolves, we were mavericks . . . actually, most people in the industry answer this description, but it makes us sound way cooler. Even though we were mavericks, lone wolves, Hilary and I worked well together. Every year we sat down and made a plan for the year and she was always asking me what my five-year plan was. Because, let's face it, at the end of the day, we all want to feed our families, we need a roof over our heads and we also want to spend some time with the family. It's not all about work and nothing else!

Festivals were always a large part of the yearly and five-year plans. I don't know many comedians who specialise in festival work in the way that I have come to do. These days, I do festivals for around six months of the year, both in New Zealand and in Australia. Since that Adelaide Fringe in 2009, I haven't missed a year on that side of the ditch, doing one or (usually) more a year. Festival season is full-on, although there can be anything from days to weeks between festivals. And it is a definite season. Around September, it winds down and, like most comedians, I make my money during the off-season from corporate gigs, where you host awards nights or conferences and that kind of thing. There's plenty of this kind of work around: every industry you can think of — from plumbing to pornography — has an awards night once a year, and they all have conferences. For the record, I've never hosted anything in the pornography sector, but I'm open to it. I mean plumbers don't plumb at the plumbing awards so I don't think porn stars will be fake-fucking at the porn awards.

I did come close. I once got an offer to go to a New Year's gig at a naturist (that is, nudist) camp. They sounded very nice in their emails, but the elephant in the room was the nudity. They wanted me to come and do a gig over midnight at the nudist camp. That was fine and dandy, but they were clear that everyone would be completely naked. They would be cool with it if I wanted to wear a toga, but they would prefer me in the raw, too.

Well, I replied to that email (copying Hilary in) saying, 'This sounds very interesting.'

Then I sent Hilary a text. 'Holy fuck can you imagine me naked in front of 300 people doing jokes?' I wrote. 'And they're naked! I wouldn't be able to yell out DICK every now and again like I've got a tic.'

"THE ELEPHANT IN THE ROOM WAS THE NUDITY. THEY WANTED ME TO COME AND DO A GIG OVER MIDNIGHT AT THE NUDIST CAMP."

Oh, we laughed! She replied, but such is the interconnectedness of all things online that she had received my text on her laptop and responded via email. 'Can you imagine these naked freaks laughing and their bits jiggling as you go?! How distracted would you be!'

This, of course, found its way into the inbox of the naked guy, so I never got to do that or any other gig in the altogether.

It would have been an experience, but in case you've slopped your highball on your privates in your haste to try to book me for your naked gig, let me just say that my answer will always be 'NO!' It's not what you think. I'm happy if you're happy to be naked, but it comes down to mosquitoes. They love me! It would be a feast for them if I got my bits out, so I prefer to cover up.

The One About THE LITTLE SCREEN

Towards the end of the 2011 season, I was in Queenstown in the South Island of New Zealand doing the Winter Festival. I was the rookie comic, the one opening for all the other well-oiled comedians who were there. The festival flew Julie and me down — it was great! It was a night of two halves, with the entertainment arranged around an interval. The comedy was first, with everyone doing seven minutes of stand-up in a gala-type set-up, except for me. I had to do 15 minutes, because I wasn't involved in the second half of proceedings. Once I had got the crowd going, I could sit and just enjoy the rest of the night, which comprised a live show of *7 Days*, a popular comedy programme screening on one of the three main free-to-air television channels, TV3.

I was just enjoying the floating feeling of relief after my

stand-up spot — which seemed to have gone down OK — when Jeremy Corbett, the host of *7 Days*, came up to me and asked if I'd seen the show before.

'Of course!' I said. 'Who hasn't? It's the number one show in New Zealand.'

'Excellent!' he replied. 'Would you mind doing it tonight?'

It turned out that two of the guys who were supposed to do the show had eaten dodgy chicken burgers, which had rendered them out of action for the forseeable future. It's an ill wind (if that's the right aphorism for this situation) and all that. I was stoked!

The show was live on stage and followed the TV format. They quickly briefed me as to how it all works: two teams of big-name Kiwi comedians compete in a number of different 'games', all intended to encourage improvised comedy based on current affairs. My team mates were Jeremy Elwood and Brendhan Lovegrove; in the other team were Michele A'Court, Paul Ego and Ben Hurley.

It was all a bit of a blur. I really enjoyed it, because, unlike stand-up, you are not alone. You have backup with you on stage, and you can bounce off the other comedians. I didn't get stage fright, which I normally do with stand-up, but I was still incredibly nervous. The whole team thing added a dynamic that was new to me in comedy, even if it was familiar from sports I had played, especially cricket. Quite apart from the usual fear of all my jokes falling flat and of being left out on stage with the audience regarding me in stony, hostile silence, I didn't want to fail and let my teammates down. But it went well, and I finished the show on a high.

What I knew and didn't have time to tell my friends on stage is that, as well as the live show, the producers had booked me to do the TV record at the end of that week. I was buzzing about that, and I was confident I would do a good job, because I figured the stage show was basically a dress rehearsal. I don't know why it never occurred to me that the TV audience would be much, much bigger. It's a good thing it didn't: I would have spent the days leading up to the recording session shitting myself.

I had been on TV before. My first ever appearance on television was on a show called *Wero* (which means 'challenge' in the Māori language) screening on the state-funded Māori Television channel. I did a two-minute interview on my coming-out story. Then, shortly after that, I did a five-minute stand-up set on *Comedy Christmas Cracker* with Rhys Darby hosting. I was petrified. I nearly puked on the front row of the studio audience as I did my set. If that set had gone horribly wrong, it would have scarred me for life and I would never have been able to do telly again. But it went well, so now I was looking forward to hitting the big time with *7 Days*.

After the live show, Julie and I had a little mini-break in Queenstown around the single show that I did. We just walked around and ate at all the amazing restaurants and said 'ooh!' and 'aah!' at all the beautiful things. I was blown away by how pretty everything was, but a part of me really just wanted to get home so I could go on *7 Days* while my confidence level was still high. The stage show had been on a Saturday. The recording session was in Auckland the following Thursday.

It was at this point that a volcano in Chile decided to pop! The Puyehue-Cordón Caulle eruption in 2011 spewed an ash cloud all over the southern hemisphere that grounded countless flights and caused chaos. I took it pretty personally. If we'd been flying with the national carrier, Air New Zealand, it wouldn't have been a problem. None of their flights were cancelled — whether because they could fly lower or their pilots or lawyers are gamblers, I don't know, but they were flying. Julie and I arrived at Queenstown airport at 8 am on Thursday morning and spent the day enviously watching happy travellers depart on their Air New Zealand flights. I watched them leave, knowing my first opportunity to be on *7 Days* was that evening and it was looking ever more doubtful that I would make it. The lily-livers at Jetstar (Air New Zealand's Australian-owned rival) had our flight on hold for much of the morning. Then in the early afternoon they cancelled it outright. It looked like my TV debut wouldn't happen that evening. If I missed this chance, who knew whether another would ever come my way?

'Fuck that,' I thought. 'There has to be a way home!'

There was a seat left on the last remaining Air New Zealand flight for the day, due out that afternoon. Julie and I did not have much money. She wasn't working at that stage and I was doing freelance writing and comedy — say no more! We weren't exactly rolling in it. We weren't even rolling on or near it. We had maxed out all but one of our credit cards, and that one had only a tiny bit of money left on it. I took it up to the Air New Zealand counter with my heart in my mouth. I explained to the lady that I had to get to Auckland and that I was supposed to be on a TV show that night. The show couldn't be rescheduled at this short notice, I explained, with tears welling in my eyes. I had to be on that flight.

She simply looked at me and said, 'There's no seats, love.'

I'm sure she could see that I was devastated. I didn't know what to do.

'Wait,' she said.

She called over another air hostess and they both studied the computer.

'Give me your credit card,' she said.

I gave it to her. She did some more tapping on the keyboard and frowning at the screen. Then she printed something suspiciously like a boarding pass.

'Go straight through security,' she said, circling the gate number and handing it to me. 'Right now.'

I had time only to give Julie a quick hug and an empty credit card. I left her there in Queenstown, neither of us sure what would happen with her. I knew she'd sort it out. I was off. I was going to be on *7 Days*, after all!

I texted the show's producers as we waited on the tarmac, telling them I would be a few minutes late for the scheduled 3 pm meeting. The plane seemed to take forever to get into the air, and by the time we arrived in Auckland it was already 3 pm. I turned my phone on and saw a string of missed calls — one of the writers had been trying to get hold of me. I was stressed to the max!

In those days, when *7 Days* was filmed in Ponsonby, we used to meet at the More FM offices on Ponsonby Road in downtown Auckland, around half an hour's drive in light traffic, if light traffic in Auckland can be imagined. I arrived in my taxi, dripping with nervous sweat. I was wearing jeans with thermals underneath and my snow boots; there hadn't been time to change. I was shown into the shabby little room that served as the meeting room, dressing room and green room in those days. We have since moved to a proper studio in the upmarket suburb of Parnell, with working air conditioning, more than one toilet, a proper kitchen, a green room and a dressing room with a make-up area and no need to sit at folding tables next to the toilet to have our dinner.

I put a clean shirt and waistcoat on, but the jeans and the thermals had to stay. I have a problem with sweating at the best of times, because I sweat when I'm nervous and I suffer terribly from stage fright. I also sweat when I'm stressed. Plus I get anxious that I'll start sweating, and when I'm anxious I sweat. And, like most people, I tend to sweat when I'm bundled up in warm clothing in a warm room, such as a cramped little dressing room or a studio under spotlights. The only thing in my favour was that it was June and not a warm night. I would have fucking melted.

The record was a marathon three and a half hours, but it passed in a blurry flash. Near the end of it, I saw Julie in the back of the studio. She had managed to get on a flight and back to Auckland, but she was a few hours after me. If I'd waited until we could travel together, I would most definitely have missed the record.

The show has an 80-strong live audience in the studio to give us something to feed off, and they seemed responsive to my jokes. The more they laughed, the more confident I felt. At the end of the show, Jon Bridges, the producer, came up to me and hugged me and said it was great.

'Now to wait for the edit and see how the public liked it!' He smiled, and walked away.

'How the public liked it?' I thought, and for the first time I realised that it didn't really matter what the studio audience had thought. The entire nation — or at least, the solid chunk who stayed home on a Friday night and chose to watch TV3 — would watch it and they would decide if they liked my work or not.

At that point, I was still naive enough to think that I would be solely judged on my work.

The One About ANTI-SOCIAL MEDIA

It was nearly midnight by the time we headed home, tired but happy, after recording my first *7 Days*. Friday morning arrived and I started telling everyone to watch me on telly that night. 'You have to watch!' I'd say.

'So guess who's on *7 Days* tonight?' I posted on Facebook. 'That's right, y'all. Get involved, watch it and let me know what you think!'

I had to do a show in a bar in the little North Island resort town of Rotorua, so I couldn't watch my first ever appearance on *7 Days* as it went to air. Well, I sort of did. The weird thing was, the bar didn't switch their TVs off while I was performing; they just muted them. People could see me on the four tellies while I was on stage and some of them yelled out that I was on both. I could see one of the screens, and I thought, 'Well, at least they didn't edit me out. It could have been worse!'

When we went for breakfast the next morning before driving home, someone yelled at me from a passing car, 'Good work last night on the show!'

My relief was immense! 'Thank God,' I thought. 'I must have gone over OK.' I had recorded the show and meant to watch it as soon as we got home. Instead of cringing at the prospect, I started to look forward to it.

By the time I got home and watched the show, I was confident and happy.

'Yup,' I thought, after I'd watched it. 'Good enough.' Not great, not awful. Just OK.

I opened my Facebook to find out what my friends thought. They were all very positive and I thought, 'That's awesome!' Best of all, a couple of days later, the producers booked me to do another *7 Days*. I couldn't believe it! 'That one went so well, they want me on again,' I thought. I was amped.

I did the second show soon afterwards, and then it happened. I got a private message on Facebook, saying, 'You are a fat fucking idiot and your accent is disgusting.'

I didn't know what to say, so I said nothing. I thought, 'I wonder if I know this person?' I didn't, of course. He was just a troll, but that was my first.

On the actual *7 Days* Facebook page, I saw comments to the effect of 'Why the fuck do you have her on?' and 'Can't stand her.'

I was a bit shaken up, but then I saw that everyone got their fair share of hate. I realised it's normal. How awful is that for a performer? You have to allocate a certain amount of time daily for some asshole with a keyboard who will send you some horrific shit just because they can. I'm telling you, some of the stuff that I've received over the years has just blown me away. It never ceases to amaze me that people will watch a TV show and get so worked up that they will go to their computer or use their smartphone, look me up, google me, find my website, then look up my contact details, click through and write me a disgusting email. I don't know whether it's worse or better than the people who are so much more pissed off with me that they will look up my PO Box details and send me old-school snail-mail hate, so that a few days after a show has aired and I'm going to collect the mail with my toddler (who loves it) I get a disgusting letter in which the vilest shit is written about me, often enough asking me to kill myself. In some ways, to be honest with you, I appreciate the snail bile more, because at least the nutter has invested some money in their little hate project.

I have probably always had haters. Twitter was still only a puppy when I started in comedy in 2008, and back then, when people hated you on Facebook, they only did it on their page. The trolls, so to speak, were not out yet. People hadn't realised how super effective the internet could make their hate. And, anyway, my sole focus back then was to not die on stage. I was intent on getting my gear right and to keep writing new material and building a strong foundation.

But then it started. Not a lot: just here and there, someone would post a clip of me online that they had recorded illegally in a club somewhere. They'd say, 'Went to a comedy club tonight. LOVED this lady.'

Well, that, of course, if you don't know, is an open invitation for that person's friends to weigh in and let you know what a 'fucked-up fat bitch' you are — but they wouldn't mind a blowjob off you. Other friends would pipe up and say, 'Nah, bro, I wouldn't fuck that pig with your dick.'

Ahahahaaha! And I thought *I* was the comedian!

I'd think, 'What the fuck does any of this have to do with my comedy? And what gives these dirty animals the right to say anything personal about me when the discussion is clearly just about entertainment?'

I have regular haters. I guess the first time I really became aware of it was when I started doing television on a regular basis. The very first time I appeared on television I might have received some hate, but I would not have known because nobody tagged me or looked me up, and I didn't have a website at that stage or a fan page. Nobody would have known where to send their hate. That also meant there was nothing positive said about me online, either. Because positive is a thing, too. You hear a lot about trolling, but you don't hear much about people being nice and positive online — there is no name for it; you don't get 'unicorned' but you can get 'trolled' — but that's not to say it doesn't happen. Even when I did my second *Comedy Christmas Cracker*, hosted this time by Jason Cook, I had no online feedback to speak of, positive or negative.

"YOU HEAR A LOT ABOUT TROLLING, BUT YOU DON'T HEAR MUCH ABOUT PEOPLE BEING NICE AND POSITIVE ONLINE . . . YOU DON'T GET 'UNICORNED' BUT YOU CAN GET 'TROLLED'"

But then things changed. I'm not sure if it was because Twitter had got bigger and bigger since its launch in 2006 and more and more people had signed up, or whether I was just all of a sudden reaching a bigger audience and people had figured out my name.

I've learned, though, never to engage with trolls. I always try to respond when someone engages with me, regardless of the medium, but I don't when they are negative, unless I think I can mess with them for a bit.

I had this interaction with one guy recently and I just chose to chat to him because I knew that he hated me for the driving show I hosted, *Road Madness*. The show was on air for maybe 15 minutes and then I got the email from him. As soon as I read it, I laughed because I realised he must have featured as one of the terrible drivers on the show. I googled him and saw that yes, he was! That made me happy, but I didn't want him to know that I knew who he was.

HIM: 'You are not even remotely funny and your voice is disgusting.' [Another one who is not keen on my voice.]

ME: 'Well done on looking me up, googling me, then going to the effort to find a contact for me and then send me some hate online. Let's assess what happened here tonight, shall we? I did my job, which is talking on telly. You are in complete control of your remote control. (I'm just assuming you are in complete control. I would like to apologise in advance if you are not in complete control.) You have all the power to change the channel, but you chose not to do that. Instead you watched the programme that I featured in (doing my job) and went out of your way to find me and put hate on me. Not once when I went to work did I think, 'FUCK, NIGEL, I'm only here to mess with you.' But what you did, well, that's just weird. What kind of dark place are you in as a human being, that a television programme and the person in it drives you so mad you have to get in contact? Personally I hope you are not married and you don't have kids, because I don't envision they would have a great life with all the hate that lives inside you. Good luck with your situation though. I'm sure you are nailing life. (I'm being sarcastic. I'm pretty sure you aren't.)

HIM: What a rant! Feel better? Pretty sure you ain't married . . . I mean, who would? The old story — fell from the ugly and overweight tree and hit every branch, huh?

[At this point, I lose all respect for haters — when they go for the obvious insult, I always expect more.]

ME: Why can't you just be normal and hate me on Facebook? Can't figure it out?

I'm not going to lie to you: it hurt like fuck in the beginning. I couldn't understand how people would go online to attack someone they don't know from a bar of soap. How dare they? Would they be that brave if they met me in person? The answer is: no, probably not. My theory is that people who attack online probably don't have friends who would otherwise pull them into line, who'll say, 'Hey, man. What the fuck is wrong with you?'

It got worse, but it sort of got better. As I've mentioned, I got bullied at school, because I was the fat kid whose parents got divorced. Ouma Ous, my grandmother (my real one, my mother's biological mother) used to say, 'Don't you worry. You will be plagued by success one day, and then you will be happy, but you will know what this bullying is all about now. This is preparing you for life, because the highest trees get the most wind.'

It's so true. I sometimes just watch the trees and they do go nuts in the breeze, those high ones. It makes me smile. Whenever a shithead sends me a letter I think, 'It's cos I'm a tree!'

I also find solace in the fact that it's not just me. Everyone who sticks their head up above the parapet gets hate mail, even Oprah! If you can hate Oprah, there's truly something wrong with you. She's literally just trying to make the world a better place. But I get it: she's a very tall tree. She's a big oak — they sway a lot in the wind. I'm no oak; I'm not a fancy tree like that. I'm just your bog-standard eucalyptus tree, tall and strong, capable of feeding loads of cuddly koalas but also extremely flammable! I always think that the people who abuse others on social media or anywhere online must be socially very awkward. I have never — and as far as I know, neither have my close friends — looked up anyone from a television show and told them that I hate their shows. It's not that I love every show I've ever seen. It's just that I exercise the power I have to not watch anything I don't like.

"EVERYONE WHO STICKS THEIR HEAD UP ABOVE THE PARAPET GETS HATE MAIL, EVEN OPRAH! IF YOU CAN HATE OPRAH, THERE'S TRULY SOMETHING WRONG WITH YOU."

I always say to my audiences at the beginning of every show that we need to be 'friendly' to each other. Put your phone down and try to make more eye contact with people. We don't do that anymore, do we? We are all so involved with ourselves and our work that there is no more 'down' time. So I'm a big believer in interacting more with people. I do make eye contact and I give the head nod and I'll even say, 'Hi. How's it going?' Like, I'll never say, 'HELLO!' I know it's creepy to hear that from a stranger, but saying 'Hi' is cool.

Well, I had been telling my audiences this for a while, but

then one night in Melbourne a couple of years ago something awful happened on the St Kilda tramline. A man got stabbed by a couple for . . . wait for it . . . making excessive eye contact! I was petrified that he may have been at one of my shows and heard me pushing everyone to be friendlier and decided to try it that very night on his way home. Maybe he locked eyes with this couple and smiled a friendly smile, just like I said he should. Then, who knows? Maybe he was tired and he zoned out and started to think about other things, like, 'I better buy bread and milk before going home. I wonder if we still have jam . . .?' Before you know it, he's making a little shopping list in his head without taking his eyes off the couple and one of them just happens to have a knife on them because it was their birthday or something and they took a knife to work to cut the cake because they work at a spoon factory where there's no knives and then he felt threatened by this guy staring at them and felt that he had to protect them both and . . . stabbed him! Maybe the husband felt like he had to do something. 'I promised to honour and protect my wife,' he's thinking, 'and here's this young guy staring, which can't be good. I have to act now!'

But I read the article and it wasn't a happy couple working at a spoon factory at all. It was nobody's birthday. It was just two crackheads who attacked a young foreign man on a tram and nearly killed him. It wasn't my fault at all.

So much for the trolls. On the flip side, I get so much more love than hate. I've received the nicest letters and emails. I've met people who have been hospitalised because they were struggling with depression and they'll say, 'You know what?

When I'm really down, I watch your clips on YouTube and it makes me smile.' One letter like that neutralises a year's worth of shit!

I've met people who have become friends through social media, people who have been to every single show that I've ever done! I met Graham Atkinson through social media. He lives in Wellington but he has seen me perform in Auckland, Christchurch and Wellington. He has had breakfast with me and my family, and he has become such a great friend and support. There are very many Grahams in this industry — people who will look me up and say, 'Hey! You rock! Let's hang out!' Of course, as much as I'd like to, I can't hang out with all of them, because, quite frankly, I'd never be home. But, in a perfect world, I'd maybe once a year have a picnic with all of them and just hang out! Yeah, maybe I'll start doing that — just pick a park and every year around Christmas, I'll put an invite out on social media and we can all have a barbecue in the park and play a bit of cricket. Not in a competitive way, you understand, just in a 'Hey, look, guys! I can play cricket really well — that's why I chose *this* as an activity for us all.'

"PEOPLE ASK ME FOR HUGS ALL THE TIME. IT'S AT A POINT NOW WHERE I FIND IT ODD WHEN I'M OUT AND NOBODY ASKS ME FOR A HUG."

People ask me for hugs all the time. It's at a point now where I find it odd when I'm out and nobody asks me for a hug. I don't mind at all. I do mind when they try to cop a feel, because that happens sometimes, and not from the group of people you are picturing right now. I'm not sure who you are picturing — and hold your horses, I'm not anxious to find out — but I know you're wrong. It's straight women. They are the worst. But 99 per cent of the time, people are super respectful and awesome.

What I am still struggling with is people asking for photos. It's not the actual photos I struggle with; it's the speech that precedes the photo. Nearly everyone sidles up and says, 'Sorry to be this person. I'm not usually the person who asks for a photo. I don't want to be naff, but could I please ask for a photo? I know you must hate it . . .'

'Fuck, no,' I always say. 'I love it!' What other job EVER in the history of humankind will you get where people will be that happy to see you that they want a photo or a hug — or both. Just not at the same time, eh? Because we can't both look at the camera and hug. And when I say 'camera' we all know I mean phone . . .

So social media might bring all the haters onto my screen, but it also gets me in touch with my fans and I'd much rather be on it than off it. The haters are few and far between. As human beings, we naturally want to know why people are being dicks to us, which is why the haters have an impact. I've learned from my time casually being on TV that bogans slinging abuse are really telling me how fucked up they are — it's always about them, not me. At the end of the day, I'm on social media to talk to people who want to see me and hear me, and so I can post photos of my dog and me in relaxing positions. Why would I ever get rid of it? Going completely off the grid won't stop the haters; it'll just make it a little harder for them to deliver their shit to my door.

*

I thought the odd cry for help in deep, deep disguise would be the extent of the hate I could receive online. But you know what they say: the worst is the things you don't even know you don't know! So, on 25 June 2018, I appeared on *Have You Been Paying Attention?* on Channel 10 in Australia. Sorry to pop the bubble for anyone who enjoys the whiff of impending disaster on live TV, but we record the show the night before, and by the time this particular show went to air in Australia at 8.30 pm, it was 10.30 pm in New Zealand and I was already home in Auckland in bed with a book. I don't have a way to watch the show live, so I always wait up and see if I get love or hate or nothing on social media: then I know how the show is going down. So here I am reading my book and my phone starts to liven up. It's on silent, but the light keeps going off and it's happily buzzing away as I'm finishing the chapter . . .

"I THOUGHT THE ODD CRY FOR HELP IN DEEP, DEEP DISGUISE WOULD BE THE EXTENT OF THE HATE I COULD RECEIVE ONLINE. BUT YOU KNOW WHAT THEY SAY: THE WORST IS THE THINGS YOU DON'T EVEN KNOW YOU DON'T KNOW!"

'The show is either going really well tonight,' I still remember saying to my wife, 'or it's going really badly, because the phone is going nuts.'

We had a bit of a chuckle, I finished my chapter and I picked up the phone.

Well, well. I was blown away. Turned out there were a lot of Colombians online and all of them were angry and gunning for me. Most were completely fucking vile, disgusting and I had no idea why they were so angry!

On the show — which is a kind of game show — there was an individual round where we each got to have a go at guessing the identity of a team from the football World Cup (which was on at the time) who were singing their national anthem. All identifying features were removed: you basically only saw their faces and heard them sing.

The host showed me a picture of a group of men with black hair who were singing in what I was pretty sure was Spanish.

'Is it Mexico, Tom?' I guessed.

'No, afraid not,' Tom replied. 'It's Colombia.'

'Oh,' I said. 'How am I supposed to know that? I couldn't see any white powder.'

Now, was it the smartest joke I've ever made? No, not by a long shot! But it was one of those stereotypical jokes you make to get a cheap laugh. If the answer was 'It's a lesbian team' I would have said, 'Well, how can I tell? I couldn't see their comfortable shoes.'

You get me? It's not smart but it's stereotypical, and that's what jokes often are, something based on shared wisdom; something we can all see, agree on and recognise. I could have said coffee, but let's face it, a lot of other countries also grow great coffee, and coffee's not that funny. So what else do we go for? The fact is — like it or not, Colombians — you are the world's number-one producer of cocaine and unless that changes, people will 100 per cent associate you with nose candy and murderous cartels. If it was the Jamaican team, I would have made a weed joke or something about bobsleighs (perhaps I liked *Cool Runnings* a little too much). If you don't want people to stereotype you, stop doing stupid shit or choose not to get offended by it!

Anyway, in the three days after the show went to air, I

got roughly 8000 death threats and people threatening me in general. They called me everything from a whore to a cocaine whore, and a lot of pig (the more artistic even produced cartoons depicting me as a pig). And it wasn't just me. They posted hate on innocent bystanders' walls, too. If anyone had ever posted anything about me online, they would find it and they would shit all over it.

> **"ON THE BACK OF THAT SHOW, I TRENDED IN COLOMBIA AND ON THEIR SOCIAL MEDIA FOR MORE THAN A WEEK."**

There was also a massed chorus in a Spanish accent calling for me to respect Colombia and to learn more about the country, which I proceeded to do. I learned it's a beautiful country, it's been ravaged by violence because of the drugs, and a lot of people have lost their lives because of the war about the drugs. I also learned that they have amazing food and coffee. And I learned some other things that not even I will repeat here. Let's just say, I think Colombia got off lightly when I free-associated it with cocaine. If I'd known then what I know now . . .

Anyway. On the back of that show, I trended in Colombia and on their social media for more than a week. I was on every news programme and sports programme, and they said I had insulted The Soccer Team (which I had not). I got loads of hate from Colombians living in Australia, with a huge hotspot being Sydney, where there's one particular guy who left Colombia for Amsterdam and then moved to Australia, where he now lives and works. He led the charge of hate against me, trying to pull together groups of Colombians to come to my shows and disrupt them. I won't reveal his whole name, but Jean and Franco are the first two, and all you really need to know is that he was a very, very septic Colombian, let me tell you. Others got over themselves, but he would not let a thing go and he sent me several death threats. I reported his Twitter account, but of course filth and death threats are what Twitter is all about, so no action was taken to block him. In the end, though, it turned out that he just went septic about a lot of things online and his widely directed threats never came to much. Still, it was nice to have extra security at the gigs for a while — not that I needed it; it was just nice to meet new people, really!

But there was one particularly dark thing that happened the week after that show. I was due to appear on the programme again, and I was aware that some of the angry Colombians had sworn to disrupt the filming. It's hard to hide from these people when you have to promote your work. I mean, you can't promote anything in secret — my upcoming dates are listed on my website because I have to sell tickets for them! So maybe I was a bit edgy when I arrived early, as per usual, into Melbourne a week after *that* show. My driver is always right there, waiting, as I exit the international customs area, but when I walked out on this day there was a new driver holding the placard with my name on it. This was strange. Up until this point, I'd only ever had two drivers who would alternate, so I was, as you can imagine, a little scared at this turn of events. I went with the new driver, who silently took my bag and walked ahead of me. As we left the airport, I was furiously texting my wife and manager, telling them both that there was a new driver and I was going to try and sneak a photo of him to show them. I had my headphones on and my head down messaging, when all of a sudden it went very dark in the car. When I looked up, we were in a tunnel. I freaked out, because I've been to Melbourne heaps of times and the drivers always take the same route to the hotel. I'm not sure I could describe the route we usually take, but I know for a fact that it doesn't have a tunnel. I didn't even know Melbourne *had* a tunnel. Something was wrong.

'WHY THE FUCK ARE WE IN A TUNNEL?' I screamed. 'WHAT ARE YOU PLAYING AT? WHERE ARE WE GOING? WHERE ARE YOU TAKING ME?'

I saw the whites of the driver's startled eyes in the rearview mirror.

'It's the shortest way,' he said, waving at the dashboard, 'according to my navigation.'

Even from the back seat I could see, true as nuts, that the electronic navigation was showing it was a shorter way! I'm not sure why none of the other drivers had ever taken me that way?! I realised I was on edge. I decided I had better calm down before the record that night.

I checked into my hotel and decided to have a nap to chill out. I stripped down (sorry if you're a graphic thinker, but yeah, I'm naked at this point: all part of the relaxation routine) and I must have fallen asleep, because nek minit there was a very loud knock on the door. I got such a fright that I basically threw myself out of the bed and yelled.

'Who is it?! WHAT-DO-YOU-WANT?'

It came out almost as one long, wailed word.

There was a pause.

Then a quiet voice came from the other side, 'Never mind. I'll come back later.'

I heard footsteps recede down the hall at the same moment I registered a searing chest pain. Both my boobs were on fire. I looked down and realised that in flinging myself from my bed, I had sustained carpet burns on both nipples. I know, right? Turns out that's a thing! I've never known such horrific pain, and I've had a kidney removed!

It was excruciating, and at this point I felt that the Colombians had won. I was still not ready — and nor will I ever be ready, so long as we have green grass, blue skies and water in the ocean — to apologise. Maybe if as an entire nation they all calmly said, 'Hey, we were offended by what you said. Please apologise.' Even then, given the way they reacted, I wouldn't apologise. Not even if the apology meant the difference between a long and healthy life or a slow horrible death by hyperthermia. I *still* would not give them the pleasure of apologising.

> **"THERE IS NOTHING, NOTHING, I TELL YOU, THAT SOME BADLY DRESSED, CHAUVINISTIC VIRGIN WHO LIVES WITH HIS MOM CAN SAY TO ME ON TWITTER THAT'LL UPSET ME MORE THAN HAVING CARPET BURNS ON MY NIPPLES."**

I have since learned that you can turn regions on or off on your social media. I have also learned that you can turn off your social media pages for a couple of weeks. It's quite nice to have a little holiday. And since the Colombian Incident of mid-2018, I've had other topics that have caused a bit of heat on social media. But honestly, after having that full-scale attack launched upon me, I'm unafraid! There is nothing, nothing, I tell you, that some badly dressed, chauvinistic virgin who lives with his mom can say to me on Twitter that'll upset me more than having carpet burns on my nipples.

And my last word for Colombians is this. As someone who has seen people lose their temper in a mall and yell at their own family, let me tell you, no one looking on thinks the family is fucked up. Everyone thinks the person doing the yelling is fucked up. So think about that, Colombians! You are the person losing your temper in the mall! (I'm sure this book won't be selling in Colombia, but if you're visiting, feel free to pass this message on.)

The One About AN AUCKLAND SCHOOLTEACHER ENDING APARTHEID

I was doing a fun bit of interactive television for Māori Television during the 2011 Rugby World Cup when South Africa was playing Samoa. I attended the game, and it was a thriller! The final score was 13–5 to South Africa, but the score didn't reflect the physicality and toughness of the game . . . Anyway. The morning of the game, I went to Otara markets in South Auckland, where the producers of the show knew there'd be a whole lot of Samoan supporters. I donned my South African supporter's kit and off we went.

It was a lovely morning. I'd bowl up to people and ask who they thought would win. I'd tell jokes, they'd tell jokes, we'd all pick our favourites to win the cup and guess who would score first — you know, light-hearted rugby stuff.

We were almost done and busy wrapping up filming when I heard, 'You are that *comedian*, aren't you?'

I turned and saw John Minto — professional protester, who was taking time out from pushing something down people's throats to talk to me — and I said, 'Yes, I am.'

He then proceeded to give me a two-minute telling-off about how South African immigrants have nothing to offer New Zealand but dried meat and don't deserve to be here, whereas the Samoans have so much to offer and give so much of themselves. White South Africans needed to leave, he reckoned, not least because they never showed any respect for the fact that New Zealand — and by inference, John Minto — single-handledly ended apartheid in 1981.

I had to stop him there.

'Did you send the end of apartheid on a Jetstar flight, pal? We didn't get it till 1994, officially!'

I had no idea what he was talking about. He explained that in 1981 New Zealand had a series of dramatic protests against the touring South African rugby union team, the Springboks, that led directly, without passing go or collecting $200, to the end of apartheid. I took that information away with me and read up about it, because I had never previously heard about the anti-tour movement or the protests. I know quite a lot of South Africans, quite a lot of whom had their ear to the ground in the 1980s and 1990s, and only two of them had heard of the protests against the 1981 Springbok tour.

This is hardly surprising (even if it might surprise and even disappoint John Minto). The government we had in 1981 was very controlling of its people. I know: amazing, right? We were told what to wear, what to watch — hell, we as a nation only got television in 1976 once the government was sure it could control what we watched, and, in the meantime, it controlled what we listened to and what we read! There was no way on God's green earth that they were going to tell us, 'Hey, guys. You won't believe this, but the outside world doesn't think we are doing a good job with our political decisions and the way we run this joint!' We had no idea.

" PEOPLE THREW FLOUR BOMBS ON THE PLAYERS. THAT LITTLE NUGGET OF INFORMATION WAS VERY DIFFICULT TO ABSORB FROM A KIWI, WHAT WITH THE ACCENTS AND EVERYTHING. "

So let's see if I've got it straight. Basically, the South African rugby team came over to play the All Blacks — bold choice to play the ALL BLACKS during apartheid — then, while they were here, there were protests. People threw flour bombs on the players. That little nugget of information was very difficult to absorb from a Kiwi, what with the accents and everything. A friend told me that they threw flour bombs on the players.

'Flower?' I asked. 'Like, daisies and shit?'

'No! Like, self-raising flour. Baking and shit.'

'Ahhh, I see. So white players come to New Zealand to play rugby and the country they were born into has an issue with black people so you throw flour on them and . . . what? Make them more white? How does that help?'

*

What I'm saying is: we didn't know any of that happened. Don't get me wrong. I think it's good to protest (NOT EVERYTHING GOING, JOHN MINTO) and you should definitely stand up for what you believe in. We should stand up for people with no voice. It's our duty as human beings, and it's what separates us from animals. But I couldn't swallow the argument that John Minto ended apartheid for us, and I still can't.

The One About THE BAG LADY

I haven't missed a year in Australia since my first visit in 2009. I've done at least one festival over there (if not more) every year and, slowly but surely, I'm getting myself a little audience. It's not a massive following by any stretch of the imagination, but let's just say that I'm no longer losing money over there. I'm playing 150-seater rooms, which might not sound big compared with New Zealand's audiences, but I'm glad I persisted, because the 'foundation' work is done and it's strong and hopefully one day I will have struck the perfect balance between performing in New Zealand and performing in Australia.

My most memorable festival to date would be the first year I did the Melbourne International Comedy Festival in 2012. I decided to go and check Melbourne out. I couldn't spare the time to do the full run, so I booked 12 shows and did a split bill with English-Kiwi Reuben Lee, a show that we called *His & Hers*. We performed in the Carpet Room at the Forum Theatre on Flinders Street, which seats around 30 people. Or, I should say, it would have seated 30 people. We literally could not give tickets away to this show. There were only ever about five people in there on any given night. The reviewers — all five of them — hated it.

"WHENEVER I DO A FESTIVAL, I GET UP IN THE MORNING, HAVE BREAKFAST AND TWO OR THREE CUPS OF COFFEE, TAKE MY BAG AND WALK THE STREETS ALL DAY PRESSING FLYERS ON PEOPLE."

Whenever I do a festival, I get up in the morning, have breakfast and two or three cups of coffee, take my bag and walk the streets all day pressing flyers on people. I stop at about 4 pm, when the other comedians come out to pass out flyers, because I don't want to compete with them. I also find people don't want your flyer when they are on their way home; they just want to get home. If they get your flyer during the day, on the other hand, they will look you up at work and sift through some of your YouTube clips. It's more effective. SECRET'S OUT, people! But, back then, I didn't have a lot of YouTube to direct people to.

One day, I had taken up a position at the top of the stairs in front of the Melbourne Town Hall, where there was a chalkboard advertising what was on that night. People would come up to look, and I'd give them a flyer and tell them to go and see my show. Well, on this particular day, a bag lady walked up to me and asked me what I was doing in front of the Town Hall.

'I'm a comedian,' I answered. 'I'm flyering.'

She took a flyer.

It was a Tuesday, so I gave her a winning smile.

'It's Cheap-ass Tuesday,' I said.

'No, no,' she said, and waved her hand as though shooing away a fly. She stalked off. 'Probably for the best,' I thought. 'If I've offended her with the word "ass", she'd never survive the show.'

That night, when our show started, there were only three people in the room. Reuben and I had collared them across the road just before the doors opened. They were mates out on the piss, and they were too drunk to refuse. We needed an audience; they'd do. We gave them free tickets. We had given away about 20 tickets, but these three were the only ones to show up. I was up first for 30 minutes. Five minutes in, the door at the rear of the room burst open and my homeless lady was standing there with a collection of bulging plastic bags.

I stopped talking. The three drunks turned, as did my sound technician.

'WHY AREN'T YOU AT THE TOWN HALL?' she asked, very agitated.

'Good question!' I replied. 'I'll check with the festival tomorrow.'

She had assumed that because I had been flyering at the Town Hall, I was performing there.

'I went to the wrong place, and now I've missed half the show,' she grumped.

'Don't worry. I'll start from the beginning,' I said, which I proceeded to do.

She sat there in stony silence. She didn't laugh once, but as I walked off after 35 minutes (leaving poor Reuben only 25), she said loudly that she liked me. Reuben had only just got started when she said, 'Wait,' got up, assembled all her plastic bags and shuffled towards the door.

'I don't like him,' she said, and the door banged shut behind her. I followed her and tried to give her a refund. It wasn't right that she — a homeless person — had bought a ticket when I'd been giving them away, but she wasn't having a bar of it. I later found out she also paid full price, and not the 'Cheap-ass Tuesday' price. It was the idea that she was being offered charity that had irritated her outside the Town Hall. I was impressed as all hell!

During that trip to Melbourne, I met Wanda Sykes. You don't know who Wanda Sykes is? Google 'Racist Dolphin', strap in and prepare to laugh yourself sick! She's a genius and a hero of mine, one of my favourite comics of all time. Whenever people ask me who my influences are or who I admire, Wanda is the first to spring to mind.

"WHENEVER PEOPLE ASK ME WHO MY INFLUENCES ARE OR WHO I ADMIRE, WANDA IS THE FIRST TO SPRING TO MIND."

Julie hadn't come with me to Melbourne, so if Reuben was otherwise occupied I was left at a loose end after my shows. One night I wandered into the festival's artist bar and ordered a beer. It was really quiet in there — only a couple of promoters sitting in one corner gossiping — and, besides me, there was only one other person at the bar. I turned to see who it was and lo and behold! It was Wanda Sykes herself, standing right next to me!

I couldn't believe it.

I turned to her and said, 'Wanda Sykes?'

She looked at me.

'I just want to say that you are an amazing comic and I love your work,' I said.

There was a pause, during which she kept looking at me. Then she leaned right into my face and said, 'FUCK OFF.'

I couldn't believe that, either.

I took my beer and fucked off promptly. I saw her again later in the night: she was celebrating or something, but I didn't try again. I put her rudeness down to the fact that she wasn't in the mood to talk to some stranger at a bar, which is fair enough. And I should say that I met Wanda again in Montreal in July 2018. She was lovely, and she said I had nice hair. All is forgiven.

Reuben and I lost money on that festival, as you can imagine. It's quite common to lose money on a festival if you aren't 'known'. We each had to pay more than AUS$1000, but the experience was worth every penny. We had a great time. We both had issues with our accommodation. (There's a theme emerging here, isn't there?) He was in a dormitory in a backpackers and I was staying with a friend who turned out to be a homophobe. Neither of us could afford better accommodation, so we just delayed going home by drinking $3 pints and chatting to other comedians. We had a ball. Every time I've been to Melbourne since, I have thought about our time there together. It was great to have a friend and a travel-

and-performance buddy all rolled into one. Being a comedian on the road is really lonely sometimes, and I take my hat off to comics who have been doing it for years. I couldn't do that. I'm too tight with my family; I need my people. My wife and kids always join me on the road now.

*

There was another sequel to that first Melbourne tour. In 2016, I was sitting in the bar of the Victoria Hotel on Little Collins Street in Melbourne telling the crew about my little old homeless lady, and how she paid full price and didn't want a refund. I finished my story and sipped my wine. There was this amazing piano music in the background.

'I wonder what music it is?' I said, and we looked around.

There she was, my homeless lady, playing the piano in the Victoria Hotel bar! I had to look her up to see who she was. Her name is Natalie and she's 83 years old as I'm writing this. She's a common sight around Melbourne and has played on many pianos throughout the city. Natalie's lost both her daughters and she's suffered from bad health and is homeless. She's had a sad life — I'd say horrible, if it was mine — and yet she plays the most beautiful music. The moment she walked into my show at the Forum will forever be one of the highlights of my comedy career. It was an honour to perform for her. It also reminded me that we're all just a couple of bad life events away from becoming lost or homeless. There but for the grace of God, and all that.

Natalie, the lady who came to my shows in
Melbourne when no one else did.

The One About CRACKING AUSTRALIA

In 2012, after returning to New Zealand from the failed Melbourne run — well, it was a learning experience, anyway, and it all went well apart from the fact we didn't actually test our gear on real, proper audiences — I did a new show called *I'm Gonna Need a Second Opinion*, all about me having cancer.

Talk about luck! Or perhaps it was more a matter of being in the right place at the right time with the right gear and attitude. Jason Byrne, who is a famous Irish comedian, and his producer Bec Sutherland, were there. Bec is the head of comedy at Live Nation, which is one of the biggest producers of anything entertainment, ever! Don't feel bad if you haven't heard of Live Nation; I hadn't, either. To tell the truth, I didn't even know what it meant to have a producer. But Bec offered to sign me up, and the difference was immediately obvious. The next year I was back in Melbourne doing a solo show — and playing the Town Hall! Sure, it was just a 60-seater room, but it's the Town Hall, baby! It's much easier building foundations when you have someone — especially someone like Live Nation — helping with the digging.

The one sadness I have — I don't waste my time with actual regret, remember — is that signing with Live Nation meant I had to say goodbye to Hilary and Creeping Charlie. The five-year plans Hilary and I pulled up together didn't fit with the path my career was taking, which more and more led to Australia, and more, and bigger, while Hils wanted family and chill. I thought we could still be friends even if we didn't work together, but we couldn't and we're not. We're no longer in communication, and it sounds silly, but it feels like the hardest break-up I've ever gone through. I still do five-year plans. It's just that now there are some pretty big-ticket items on there, and it's thanks to Bec and Live Nation that I've achieved many of them (did I mention Netflix? I did? Well, we're getting to that . . .).

In 2016, I found myself back in the Forum Theatre — not in the Carpet Room, this time, but playing the downstairs room, which seats 400. I didn't sell it out, but I had 300 in there, so I was feeling pretty chuffed with myself. The Carpet Room will always be close to my heart, just like the Vault at Q Theatre in Auckland. The Vault only seats a few people, but, by god, were people generous in attending those shows I had in there — so generous I had to move out of that room. I outgrew the Vault just as I outgrew the Carpet Room, and you can't help but think fondly of the rooms and the audiences that helped you do it.

In 2018, the boomerang of luck that is my career took me back to the Forum again. This time I played the newly refurbished big room, which seats 800 people, and I sold it out my entire run. I added three extra shows in there and one additional show in the main Town Hall in Melbourne. Whatever happens, I'll always think fondly of the colourful and iconic old Forum. In many ways, it's where it all began for me, if we're talking about my international success — and really, what's the point of talking about anything else?

By the time I signed up to Live Nation, I still hadn't really done anything on television in Australia, but I was doing as many festivals as I could and the rooms were steadily getting bigger. I'd done a few galas for the Melbourne International Comedy Festival, but those were all one-offs and nothing that stuck, like *7 Days* in New Zealand stuck to me. In 2016 I did my show *Man Up* at the Swiss Club on Flinders Lane in Melbourne. It was a 150-seater and, after every show, I would walk out and greet the audience and thank them for coming. We'd have a laugh and if they wanted, we'd have a photo. My run sold out and I had the most amazing time; I had to add a few shows, which as a performer is the best feeling in the world! After one of those nights, waiting for the crowd, I had a woman walk up and shake my hand. She introduced herself as Susannah. She said she was a producer and gave me her card.

'I've got a TV show,' she said. 'I'd like you to come and check it out.'

The clouds split and a shower of golden tickets to Hollywood fluttered down around me: not. I had already learned by then that it usually doesn't work out that way. A lot of people call their podcasts a 'radio show', and if they shoot a clip off their iPhone on a tripod, they call it a 'TV show'. So naturally, I was sceptical. I smiled and nodded and took her card. And luckily, I ran it past Bec to see what she thought.

She studied the card for a moment. Then she smiled.

'It's legit!' she said. 'Get into it!'

So I rang Susannah and we set up an appointment, and I went and watched the show. It was a quiz show called *Have You Been Paying Attention?* (yes, the one of Colombian Incident fame, but that would come later) and there were five participants. By the look of it, these comprised two radio guys, a TV person and a comedian or two . . . it looked like just my cup of tea, and I got booked to do the show. Then, let's just say . . . the clouds split open and golden tickets to Hollywood fluttered down around me. I fell in love with that show right off the bat and the show loved me back. We bonded, and it was a thing of beauty! As of late 2018, I've been doing the show for three years without looking back. The guys who started it and who are the show's regulars, Sam and Ed, are just the best guys. The host, Tom, is the glue that keeps it together. It hardly matters who's on: it's always a great show and people love it.

Thanks to the profile that *Have You Been Paying Attention?* gave me, I've since started working on a variety of other shows in Australia, from *Orange is the New Brown* (with my good friend Nazeem Hussain) to spots on *The Project* in both Australia and New Zealand (in fact, and correct me if I'm wrong, I believe I'm the first person to have done both Projects). I've also been on *Hughesy, We Have a Problem* and *Get Krack!n*, and I've even made a short film with some mates that made it to the finals of Tropfest in 2018.

It doesn't get much bigger than that, darl.

THERE'S THESE TWO LESBIANS WHO WANT TO HAVE A BABY . . .

So we're sitting there, Julie and me, nice and comfy on the couch in our rental house in Blockhouse Bay with the phone on the coffee table in front of us. We've made a few calls already, and the response has been encouraging. We phoned Julie's nan first, and she was overwhelmed, delighted, everything we knew she would be. We phoned her parents next. They were pretty happy, too. Then we started to work our way through the siblings. Of course, I'm not going to lower myself into a world of shit by setting down the order in which we phoned people. Do I look stupid? Let the record show we phoned everyone who we thought would want to share in the joy, and all that crap.

So we phoned Julie's sister, who lives in Brisbane. There's a bit of chit-chat, you know, small talk. Then we cut to the chase.

'We're going to have a baby,' Julie tells her sister.

'Oh my god!' she says, and there's a short pause. 'Was it a planned pregnancy?'

"AS A COMEDIAN, YOU OFTEN FEEL LIKE SOME KIND OF OLD-TIME PROSPECTOR TRUDGING THROUGH A BARREN WILDERNESS, STUDYING EVERY NO-GOOD ROCK IN THE LANDSCAPE FOR SIGNS OF PAYDIRT."

As a comedian, you often feel like some kind of old-time prospector trudging through a barren wilderness, studying every no-good rock in the landscape for signs of paydirt. Then, every now and again, you stumble across a nugget. A big, fat, gleaming nugget of pure fucking comedy gold amongst all the dust and dross.

This is how I do that moment in my show:

My wife and I have a baby . . . [I pause here.]

I'll let that sink in for a minute. I want you to think about it for a second, because I need you to know that it was a planned pregnancy . . . very planned.

[There's usually a few laughs at first, then more, as people catch on.]

Because when we started ringing the family to tell them that we were expecting a baby, we rang her sister, who now lives in Brisbane, Australia, to tell her that we were expecting. As soon as we told her, she asked, 'Oh my god! Was it a planned pregnancy?'

[I look mockingly over my shoulder to the empty stage behind me to see if commonsense is hiding in the room. I

look, confused, back at the audience. Then I say, kind of off-topic] Now, I don't know how much oxygen they've got in Brisbane. But I don't think it's enough . . .'

[I usually pause for a few laughs, especially in Melbourne.]

Was it a planned pregnancy? What the hell? I said, 'No. No, it wasn't planned at all. The dildo exploded . . .'

[I usually have to pause for quite a while at this point, even if only to keep my own composure.]

We're expecting Tupperware in August!

I should state right now that the reason Julie denies this ever happened, or has blocked it out, is that we both face-palmed so hard that she may have knocked it right out of her memory bank. Either that, or she wants to divert attention away from that sister. Sometimes she goes on the counter-offensive and claims it was my sister. She could be right, but she's not. In my show, I add 'She's a doctor!' but that part isn't true. Julie's sister used to work for Inland Revenue in New Zealand before she shifted to Australia. Now she's in Accounts Receiving or something. Julie loves her sister and doesn't want me to share this episode too widely, so I've kept it between you and me and whoever else has packed out my gigs in New Zealand and Australia since it happened. I didn't resent the question, any more than a prospector would resent it if you tapped him on the shoulder and said, 'There's a real shiny rock just over there.' Keep those dumb-ass questions coming, I say! Lucky for me, this whole area — childbirth and lesbyterianism — has proved to be a regular goldmine of dumb-ass questions.

Second prize in the tragi-comic responses to our news

stakes was Elinor, Julie's mom. When we told her, the speakerphone was quiet for a moment as she grappled with what she was feeling.

'Ah,' she said. 'Another one born out of wedlock.'

The speakerphone was quiet at both ends while we all grappled with what we were feeling.

'Well, to be fair, Elinor,' I said after a while, 'we would have avoided having a bastard child if it was legal for us to marry. But it's not!'

Julie and I weren't about to put our lives and dreams of having a family on hold because of some stupid law preventing us from getting married. We agreed early on that we wouldn't have a civil union. Why do something that legally means jack shit but costs just as much as a real wedding? Hell, no.

Anyway. So, as I may have mentioned, our pregnancy was planned, as the pregnancies of gay couples tend to be. I'm not about to go into the details of the planning, any more than I'm going to go into the details of the execution. I know this will come as a considerable disappointment to many of you, if not most of you. Because the most common line of dumb-ass questioning is where we got sperm from and how did we get it up there?

'Did you go old-school?' people ask, nudge-nudge, wink-wink. If they are too up-front for innuendo, they just ask whether I got a guy in to fuck my partner. While I'm not going to go into details, let me state for the record that no, no one came in to 'service' my partner.

Credit where it's due, people are amazingly comfortable talking about it. I was talking to a friend of mine one day, and we were just having a chat. This friend cuts her own fringe. You don't NEED to know that, but I'm just being open and honest about it, in the same way people were open and honest about our pregnancy. So I'm talking to my friend and her fringe is looking particularly bad that day. It's never that pretty. It's like she's punishing herself when she cuts it. But today, on the day in question, it's so uneven that she'll have to shave a couple of centimetres in to even it out.

Do I say anything? No, of course I don't! I was raised right!

Nobody in our circle of friends ever says anything to her about the bad haircuts she insists on giving herself. It puzzles us all, and we bleed for her every time we see her looking as though she was washing her hair in the sink when the waste disposal got turned on. It's not a money thing; she can afford a professional hairdresser. She just thinks she does a good job, and who are we to tell her otherwise?

Anyway. I'm talking to her and a mutual friend walks up to come and chat with us. I see her see the fringe. I know she has seen the fringe, because she rolls her eyes wildly when she looks at me. Now, instead of addressing the fringe, she just kind of looks at me with a 'save me from talking about that fringe' look, points at my vagina and asks, really loudly, 'Where *did* you girls get sperm from?'

That has the effect of making the friend with the fringe and everyone around us also look at my vagina, as though the answer to this and to all the other prurient questions they might have are actually written there.

I would like to say I'd never been so uncomfortable in my life, but alas! I've been way more embarrassed than that in public by my weird friends.

So, when I say that people are quite open and honest about lesbyterian pregnancy, I mean they are actually rude and intrusive. But I don't mind any of it. I don't mind the weird questions or the pointing or even some of the prejudice because there's an old saying that 'all is grist to the mill'. Like you, I don't know what grist is, but I know it when I see it. I can talk about this stuff on stage, I can make it funny and I can make people think about it — perhaps even to question their own stupid beliefs.

> **"COMEDY CAN BE QUITE POWERFUL LIKE THAT: IT'S THE VELVET GLOVE AROUND THE IRON FIST OF THE TRUTH."**

Now this is the bit I love about being a comedian. I don't get offended by stuff. It makes me want to talk to you about it. Not personally, mind; just from the stage. And, if I can make my point in a calm way and get you to see that, ah, the gender of the parents doesn't matter, as long as they love the child, and who knows, maybe you even leave happy and more open-minded, I'm happy. Of course, if you still can't budge on your opinion, then you can fuck right off, but I do think most people listen a bit. Comedy can be quite powerful like that: it's the velvet glove around the iron fist of the truth.

Because this is the strangest thing of all. A lot of people can be as open-minded as you like. They will accept gay people, transgender, bi — you name it, whichever part of the alphabet you associate with, they will support you and never give you an ounce of shit. But the minute there are kids involved, then it's like those same level-headed, normal people lose their minds!

'KIDS?! YOU ARE HAVING KIDS?! Fuck, no! Kids need a mother AND a father!'

I wrote a bit of comedy about it. Now, just a note of caution. This bit is pure fiction, people! It never happened, but I can see how it *could* happen and that's how my comedy works. Also I needed to write it to work in with how close-minded people think, so I had to drag Geoff, my father-in-law, into this gag, even though none of this has ever been uttered by him. Please, don't put hate on the old guy who, as I say, never said what I am about to say he said. This is the gag about having same-sex parents that I use occasionally.

> *As soon as we told people we were expecting a baby, everyone asked the same question: 'Who's the father?' To which we always said, 'There's no father. There's just two mothers.' Then they'd say, 'Yeah, I hear you. But who's the father? You know what I mean.'*
>
> *Yeah, I do know what you mean, but there's no father!*
>
> *My father-in-law is the worst. He is always at us, going, 'Who's the dad? If there's no dad then this kid is fucked!'*
>
> *I always say, 'That's such horse shit! I grew up with no dad, raised by a single mother and I'm fine . . .'*
>
> *Then you can see him think. [I make a* tick-tick *noise with my hand, showing the mechanical working in the brain.] He yells, 'THAT'S WHY YOU'RE GAY!'*
>
> *He's so proud of himself. You can see he thinks he's nailed it. I say, 'OK, well, let's completely forget that your daughter is gay too and she grew up with you! And she's* very *gay — she's gayer than me, quite frankly! Let's totally forget that! Because I know that there will always be the percentage of people anywhere at any time in any country that thinks if there's no dad then the kid will be gay. If you truly believe that is true, if you truly truly believe that, then the whole of [insert the name of any shitty town, city or*

suburb where single mothers are in abundance — I often use Moe in Victoria where, let's face it, Father's Day is the most confusing day of the year] must be FABULOUS! You drive through there and it's just rainbows and butt plugs and confetti cannons going off all day! Get real!'

Now, people laugh at that, but I know that most of them will know someone who really holds that completely wrong and fucked-up view. But if they can start laughing next time their idiot of an acquaintance spouts that stupid shit, and say, 'Hahaha, you must think Moe is fabulous, then!' a conversation might get started. I reckon that's how we stop hate — if the rest of us can genuinely laugh at the idiots who spout it. Laughter and honesty is also how I reckon we will combat bullying in schools.

The One About THE JOY OF CHILDBIRTH

Finding out Julie was pregnant was truly one of the happiest days of my life. I jumped up and down in the house yelling, 'We're gonna be mommies!'

Julie and I knew from the get-go we both wanted kids. We decided that, since my job entailed lots of travelling around, she should be the one who got knocked up and stayed at home. We also thought we should buy a house. As mentioned, my own childhood had been spent as a nomad roaming from place to any other place where my deadshit dad hadn't got pissed and alienated everyone by getting into a fist fight, or showing up to work drunk, so that he would be home before lunchtime and telling us we were moving right away. I was lucky; it hadn't affected me much, but I'm pretty sure a lot of Quintin's issues were down to the fact that every time he got even remotely settled, it was time to run away again, leaving yet another school and another set of friends behind him. He went to 11 primary schools in the end. We were, as mentioned, dirt poor, partly because Mom refused to ask for handouts of any kind. I didn't want that for my child. I wanted a forever home. I wanted roots. I want her to always know where she grew up — I wanted her to be able to say: 'Where did I grow up? Where my moms still live today, of course.'

I guess I might have internalised every stupid romcom I've ever seen where the adult kids go home for Christmas and their rooms are still there, the way they left them 20 years before, untouched like they'd gone missing or something.

> ***"I WANTED THE KIND OF FOREVER HOME THEY HAVE IN THE MOVIES, AND I THOUGHT WE'D HAVE PLENTY OF TIME TO BUILD THAT DREAM."***

I know the reality is very different. I know in reality, even in your forever home, as soon as you move out, your parents are making your room into the movie room, or a hobby room, or maybe putting up a fuck swing and finally living out their fantasy of a swingers club in suburbia. (I'm sorry if I just put that picture of your wrinkly parents on a fuck swing into your head.) Anyway. I wanted the kind of forever home they have in the movies, and I thought we'd have plenty of time to build that dream.

The doctor we consulted — along with Google, which we consulted to make sure the doctor was right — encouraged us to believe that it would be a long haul trying to get Julie pregnant. It took most people two years, but it took others longer still. I thought we'd have forever to save up for a house.

It didn't work out that way, oh no, because that wife of mine, Ole Fertile Myrtle there, took straight away, first go. Everything had to happen in a rush. We scratched up a deposit and bought a house in Ranui in West Auckland. (Actually, it's in Henderson, which is right next to Ranui, but I say Ranui on stage because it's a funnier suburb than Henderson. If you know West Auckland, you'll understand: it doesn't really translate into Strine, but I guess Ranui is to Henderson what Sydney's Merrylands is to Parramatta.) We are still in the same house today and Number One's room is still her room and she needs to get in there and pick up the toys!

Anyway. The pregnancy went really well. Julie bloomed and swelled and didn't suffer a minute's morning sickness along the way. It was just so exciting as the big day got closer.

Then the big day finally came. And went. Nothing happened. We all checked our watches.

The 2013 NZ International Comedy Festival was on, and I was booked to do a bunch of shows. Julie went into hospital to have an induction, so I sat with her while they administered the prostaglandin gel that is supposed to get things moving.

Nothing happened.

It got later and later in the day until I couldn't wait any longer. I kissed her and headed off to the venue. I arranged to have a table with my phone on it beside me as I performed, and I explained to the audience that my partner was in hospital and we were waiting for our baby to arrive. If I got the call, I told them, I'd have to go but I'd leave notes on stage and would pick someone out of the audience to come up and do the rest of the show because having babies was expensive and I sure as shit wasn't giving refunds!

The audience laughed obligingly, but plenty of them tried to make themselves just a little bit smaller in their seats.

I got to use the same line for two weeks running, because nothing was happening with Julie. Even when they tried a second round of prostaglandin and tipped something called syntocinon into her, she just wouldn't go into labour. By now, they were starting to get worried about the baby's placenta, which seemed to be failing. The decision was made to do a caesarian section.

The operation was performed on a Friday morning, and I was there when, to the huge relief of her moms, Number One made her grand entrance, fashionably late, and well and happy.

The One About NOT GETTING MARRIED

I never really wanted to get married. 'It's so expensive,' I used to say, and, besides, I was never keen on involving others — notably the government — in my life/love who have nothing to do with either of them. Why do I need to apply for a licence to get married? Also, why are wedding cakes so expensive?!

Right from the moment we started dating, I told Julie that she should never do anything silly like propose to me, even though I knew she really wanted to get married. She didn't seem to have given up on the idea. Soon after we got together — it must have been about 2009 — I did a gig in Thames with one of New Zealand's best comedians, Ewen Gilmour, who I'd met at the Classic. I came off stage to find Julie and Ewen in the kitchen planning our wedding and how it could be done so that it was a surprise wedding but with both of our families present. I put a pretty quick stop to all that nonsense. I was never going to get married.

Besides, in the early days, there was the small matter of it being illegal. New Zealand legalised gay marriage in April 2013. Amazing, eh? Amazing that it took so long for little old open-minded, progressive New Zealand, first in the world to give women the vote, to reach the point where we thought it was OK for people to formalise their relationship with the person they loved, no matter their gender or preferences. We were the thirteenth nation to do it. Once that obstacle was out of the way, I was the sticking point.

"SO WE GOT MARRIED. I LOVE JULIE. IT WAS IMPORTANT TO HER, WHEREAS I COULD TAKE IT OR LEAVE IT. SO WHY NOT, IN THE END, GIVE HER WHAT SHE WANTED?"

So we got married. I love Julie. It was important to her, whereas I could take it or leave it. So why not, in the end, give her what she wanted?

We had been together for six and a half years. It was hard to imagine I would ever feel as committed to anyone else on earth. So I looked up a jewellery store in Wanaka, where I was due to travel for work and chose a ring. Julie, our daughter (who was three months old by now) and I travelled to Wanaka, and bubs and I dropped into the shop to pick it up while Julie had a massage and a facial. We had dinner, and as the sun was setting over Lake Wanaka — arguably one of the most beautiful places on earth — we got out of the car in which the baby was sleeping peacefully. I produced the ring and asked Julie to marry me.

She couldn't believe it, and we both had a bit of a cry, but she actually said yes. We decided we would get married in a year's time, in November 2014.

We did the planning in bits and bobs, as 2014 was one of my busiest ever years in comedy. I travelled a lot and we had to fit the rest of our lives in between trips. We even did the rehearsal 10 weeks before the wedding, because that was the only time when a window in my schedule aligned with that of our celebrant, none other than our good friend and Julie's co-conspirator on the whole wedding thing, Ewen Gilmour.

We were really close to Ewen. His mum lives around the corner from us, so we would see him every week. He would stop by every Tuesday and have a drink and a chat and a play with the baby, who he adored and who adored him. The rehearsal — a full run-through with Ewen and his dog, Rupert — went really well. It was still 10 weeks away but we were all looking forward to the big event. It was going to be great.

On Friday 3 October, six weeks before the wedding and four weeks after the rehearsal, I was at home getting ready for a photo shoot at my house. I was quite excited and nervous. I don't like having people at my house who aren't close friends or family, so I was expecting a challenging day ahead. I had no idea how challenging it was about to get.

It was 7 am and my phone rang. It was Hilary Coe, who was still Ewen's manager at Creeping Charlie. The fact that she was calling early wasn't unusual, but it was the first time she'd called as early as 7 am. I assumed she was calling to check if I had everything under control for the shoot.

Julie was in the kitchen doing dishes and the baby was in her high chair playing with a spoon and I was walking past the kitchen with the cordless and smiling at them when Hilary asked me if I knew where Ewen's mum lived.

I registered that her voice sounded weird.

'Yes,' I said. 'What's wrong? Oh god, no.'

I thought something had happened to Ewen's mum. He was so close to her, I knew it would be tough on him if the worst had happened.

'Can you go to her house now?' Hilary asked, her voice definitely strained.

'Yes. Yes, of course I can,' I said. My mind was already racing ahead to meeting Ewen at his mum's house and being there for him in what would be a terrible time for him.

'Good,' said Hilary. 'This is going to be very hard for her.'

I was confused. She was getting it all wrong.

'Ewen died last night,' she said, choking on the words.

'FUCK OFF!' I yelled. 'DON'T TELL ME THAT SHIT!'

I couldn't believe it. My ears didn't want to hear it.

'Don't fucking lie to me. This is not funny.'

But I knew, I knew by her voice and I could hear she was crying. This is a woman who had been friends with Ewen for more than 20 years. She was floored.

I told Julie, and she started crying. The baby dropped her spoon and started crying, too. I didn't want her to stop crying. I wanted her to cry with her mommies. I left them, drove to Ewen's mum's house and just sat outside in my car, crying.

For the rest of the morning, I felt like I was walking through wet tar. My brain and my heart weren't on the same page. They hardly felt like they were in the same body. Then Julie phoned and said the make-up artist and the photographer from the magazine had arrived.

I tried to cooperate. The make-up artist would start doing my make-up. I would cry it off and she would start all over again. In the middle of all of this madness, I had news agencies phoning me for comment and television stations showing up at my house. Hilary was on the phone with me constantly telling me what was going on, what to do and who to avoid. Finally she said I had to talk to TV3. I was to send the photographer and everyone else away from my house. This wasn't a problem, because at this point the make-up lady had already packed up her bags and declared the whole thing pointless. She was upset, too. Everyone was upset. Everyone knew Ewen: he was a national treasure. We rescheduled the shoot.

Hilary told me to meet her in town at The Classic Comedy Bar in Queen Street, where she had directed all of the media people who wanted to do interviews about Ewen's life. I told her I didn't want a bar of it, but she pointed out that if I didn't do it then some industry asshole who didn't really know him would do it instead. She told me to get my ass in the car and she would meet me there.

That was hands-down one of the toughest days of my life, but I couldn't even imagine what his family was going through. To have lost him so suddenly, so unexpectedly must have been absolutely devastating, especially for his mum, Janet, who he adored. They had a very special bond, probably because his father died young at 51. Ewen was always talking about her, and took her to gigs.

And there wasn't a conversation we ever had where Ewen didn't say something about Cathy, his wife: she was the one and only true love in his life. With her, Rupert and his motorbikes, he was a very happy man. His heart took a big hit when Cathy died and I think he never really recovered from that. In the end, his heart just gave out.

His funeral was very sad and he was buried next to Cathy, which was beautiful. Hilary did the service, which was amazing. I have no idea how she held it together on the day. I looked around the massive crowd that had showed up and there were police officers, comedians, gang members, bikers, housewives, businesspeople, religious people, elderly people, youngsters — you name them. Everyone was crying, but Hilary kept it together and she kept the family away from the media and just managed the shit out of the day. It was impressive, to say the least. I know she fell apart afterwards at home, but she was a trooper on that awful day.

After the funeral, when everything had settled down, Julie and I had a conversation. We were getting married in four weeks, but we had no celebrant. We had to make a plan. It was common knowledge that Ewen was going to marry us, so we had hordes of celebrants offering to do it. I can't begin to tell you how amazing that was, but I wanted to get married only with people we knew. If we couldn't manage that, then I reckoned we should get married in front of a Justice of the Peace or whoever and have the party as planned. I knew, regardless of whatever plans we made, that we were all going to weep through the wedding. It was going to be a tough, bittersweet day.

It was then that Justine Smith's husband, Dan Crozier, a good friend of Ewen's, stepped up. Ewen had helped him become a celebrant so he could marry friends of theirs, and he said he would marry us if we liked. He and Justine were on holiday in the States at the time, and all I would have to do is change their tickets for them so they got back to New Zealand a day earlier. That was no problem at all.

Our wedding wasn't massive. We had 80 people there, which might sound like a lot, but Julie's got a big family and most of them live in New Zealand. From my side, I had the Elliotts (who count as family) and Reinette and, of course, my mom.

It was raining on the day. It pissed down, non-stop, some of the worst weather I've seen in my life. We had a

> **"I STILL MISS EWEN A LOT, ESPECIALLY TUESDAYS, WHEN HE'D COME IN BAREFOOT, USUALLY IN SKINNY BLACK JEANS AND HIS BOWLING SHIRT, SCOOP UP THE BABY AND MAKE HER LAUGH WHILE I MADE US A DRINK."**

picture of Ewen and a bottle of his favourite beer on the bar, and a few times during the day each of us just went and stood and had a moment with the photo. Ewen was meant to walk me in in place of my dropkick dad and my absent brother (Quintin approved, but even though he's had a couple of his own, he doesn't do weddings), so I had no one to give me away. My plan was to walk in with our daughter, but that was far from ideal because she was not a walker, being still at the butt-shuffling stage. And anyway, as soon as I walked in and saw Dan where Ewen was supposed to be standing, I started crying. I was fine about that. I wanted to miss him. I didn't want the day to be just glorious or to avoid thinking about him. He was mentioned over and over in the speeches, and there wasn't a dry eye in the house. There were quite a few

Me and Ewen, less than a month before he died. I loved him and he was an absolute rock in my life.

industry people at the wedding who knew him, of course, and they also knew that he was supposed to marry us.

I still miss Ewen a lot, especially Tuesdays, when he'd come in barefoot, usually in skinny black jeans and his bowling shirt, scoop up the baby and make her laugh while I made us a drink. I miss him and my wife misses him, but I'm glad she knew him, too, so that we can miss him together and tell our daughter about this great guy who she met but won't remember, and how he really wanted kids but she had to do as a substitute.

I miss Ewen. I never even got to tell him the one about the cake. He would have enjoyed that one.

The One About THE CAKE

I sometimes talk about my wedding cake in my show. I didn't want to tell the cake bakers that it was for a gay wedding, simply because I've heard horror stories from other gay couples who have ordered cakes and had really shitty service because the ladies baking the cakes haven't got fully up to speed with marriage equality at the same rate as the rest of the community.

I once went to a gay wedding where the cake shop, when they heard the request for two brides atop the cake, decided that, instead of getting two brides, they'd just cut a couple of cheap cake toppers in half and glue the two brides together so that one faced one way and the other little plastic bride faced the other way. They finished off this personalised service by basically ramming the custom cake topper up to the eye sockets in the cake. I looked at that sad little arrangement and thought, 'Good hell! That's not what I want for my wedding at all!'

So when it came to our wedding we ordered a three-tier lemon cake. We went and tasted every cake at the shop for two weekends in a row and chose the lemon cake. OK, I'll come clean. The very bottom layer was chocolate. I know it clashes, but I don't give a shit: Mama wants chocolate, so Mama gets chocolate!

So we had the cake, but we told them not to put anything up top, as I knew someone who would make us a special cake topper. In truth, at that point, we still didn't know anyone but we were looking feverishly, and finally we found Miss Bon Bon in our own area. Miss Bon Bon takes photos of you and then makes little caricatures of you to put on your cake, and that's what she did for us. She even took a photo of our daughter to put on the cake — we made her sit because at that point she still couldn't walk. Miss Bon Bon was lovely. I had no idea if she was any good and, quite frankly, I didn't give a shit. I just didn't want the about-facing, quicksand double-bride situation I'd seen before.

Miss Bon Bon called us a couple of weeks before the wedding to come in and check out the merchandise, so I went and looked at the cake toppers. She's so good, she's so gifted, those cake toppers looked so realistic and so like us that mine even had back fat! I was amazed! Amazed, and scared. My caricature was so lifelike that I feared for the lemon cake. I was scared that little cartoon me would sink into the cake and destroy it. And that's just me! I hadn't even seen the wife and kid yet. So the cake-topper lady suggested I ask the cake lady to make the cake stronger. I went back to the cake lady, who simply suggested going for a fruit cake . . . I didn't want fruit

Our wedding cake, with the heavy cake toppers. You will notice my side of the cake on the lean — I'm slowly sinking.

cake, because I'm not 100 years old. I don't know why elderly people like fruit cake, but I'm not there yet. So I stuck to the cake as ordered, and took the heifer cake toppers home and decided to pop them on the cake as late as possible on the day to delay the start of the sinking process. Of course, the risk remained that halfway through the ceremony, I would look over and think, 'Where the fuck am I? It'll only be when we cut the cake that we realise I've sunk to the second tier.'

"THAT LITTLE FAT THING WITH THE MICROPHONE WAS, OF COURSE, ME, AND I HAD INDEED STARTED CRUSHING THE TOP LAYER."

I did start sinking into the cake. My mother, who was in charge of keeping an eye on the cake, came up to me at one point and said, 'That little fat thing with the microphone on your cake is sliding off.' That little fat thing with the microphone was, of course, me, and I had indeed started crushing the top layer. We had to proceed quickly to the cutting of the cake.

Now, you might be doubting the veracity of all this, but would I lie to you? All of this is true and all of it really happened, as you can see by the photo opposite. The lesson here is that it's not really that hard to write comedy: just keep your eyes open for the crazy shit that happens in your life! I've had loads of people laugh about that story, and it's posted on my Facebook page as 'Gay Cake'. People think I've made it up, so I've since posted the photo as well and the number of people who have been in touch, saying, 'Oh my god! I thought you were just making up a joke — the fact that it really happened made me lose my shit completely!'

The Unfunny One ABOUT NUMBER TWO

So here I am, a lesbian, lesbyterian, dyke (don't like that term), queer (definitely don't like that one, because I don't think it's weird or bizarre to be gay), gay, homosexual — call it what you will, I live in suburbia with my wife and children and our dog.

We knew we wanted another child. We had got very cocky about the whole reproduction thing, because Julie got pregnant so quickly the first time. We held off when we wanted the second one, because we thought she would do the whole Fertile Myrtle routine again. Well, to cut a two-year-long story short, it didn't work out that way. By the time she conceived again, we were beginning to wonder if she ever would, and that's why we were over the moon when it happened. Number One was absolutely stoked to be a big sister. She was ready for it, going around telling everyone there were babies in everyone's tummy. It was adorable, while it lasted.

I'll remember 15 October 2015 for a number of reasons. Julie and I were having a great day, and the night before I had hosted a comedy show at the Classic. John Bishop showed up! Yes, *the* John Bishop. He was in New Zealand after a tour

"THERE ARE FEW THINGS MORE AWESOME IN THIS LIFE THAN WHEN YOU MEET ONE OF YOUR HEROES AND THEY TURN OUT TO BE AS AMAZING AS YOU ALWAYS HOPED THEY'D BE."

of Africa, where he was doing work with Comic Relief. I've always adored him. His style on stage is so calm and inviting — you just want to be his friend as soon as he starts to talk. Now, I knew he was coming — it was whispered in my ear, all secret squirrel, just days before. He was in New Zealand to do a few shows and I knew Julie loved him, so I took her with me. We got photos with him and he even signed the wall at the Classic and wrote my name in the message. I was over the moon, and then he gave us tickets to go and see him on the Friday night! Free tickets, from the man himself! There are few things more awesome in this life than when you meet one of your heroes and they turn out to be as amazing as you always hoped they'd be, because, as the first Wanda Sykes episode shows, it doesn't always turn out like that.

We were back at home on the evening of 15 October and playing with Number One, still buzzing about meeting John Bishop and how nice he was. Dinner was in the oven, Julie was pregnant and all was right with the world. We went in and had dinner — still talking about John Bishop, and how Julie and I were going to have had two dates in one week after we'd been to the show on Friday — when Julie went to the bathroom and called out to me. I went in, and there was blood, lots of blood. Julie looked terrified. I called a friend to watch Number One while we went to the hospital.

I think both of us knew it was over before we got there, and both of us were aware of the cruel irony of it: losing a pregnancy on 15 October, International Pregnancy and Infant Loss Remembrance Day. We'd been talking about it only that happy, buzzy morning.

> **“ON THE DAY WE LOST NUMBER TWO, THE THING THAT CAUGHT ME OFF GUARD WAS, YES WE LOST THE BABY, BUT THERE WAS NO SUPPORT.”**

We were shattered. I'd only once been this sad in my life and that was when Ouma Wylie died. On the day we lost Number Two, the thing that caught me off guard was, yes we lost the baby, but there was no support. The vibe from everyone was, 'Oh, well. Harden up. Plenty more where that came from.'

We went to the same hospital where our daughter was born only two years before. We arrived at the emergency room and the nurse on duty asked my wife what was going on. Julie told her that she was spotting when she went to the toilet.

'How far along are you?' the nurse asked, very blasé, and there were other questions of that sort. How many times have you been pregnant? How much blood was there? Have you ever lost a pregnancy before?

She took us out the back and showed us into a room, where a young doctor came in and took a vial of blood from Julie and left. After approximately 30 minutes, during which I was trying my very best to reassure Julie that everything would be fine, that she was not to worry, that I was getting a good vibe, all the while praying and crying myself, the young doctor came back in.

'You know, it's pretty clear you're losing this pregnancy. Your HCG Levels [human chorionic gonadotropin, a hormone produced by the placenta] levels are dropping. It's much lower than it was last week, and last week it wasn't great either. I don't think this pregnancy was ever great!'

Julie and I both started crying. He looked genuinely shocked. He walked over and awkwardly rubbed Julie's shoulder and said, 'I'm sorry. I'll leave you to it, but you are free to go home and try again later. You will need to let this pregnancy run its course and come back tomorrow for a check up.'

When we finally felt ready to leave the hospital, it was after midnight. We were tired, in shock and completely drained emotionally. At this point, I didn't think it was possible to go down a darker hole as a couple, but the night was still long and there was more to come.

When I'm sad, it presents as anger, and when I'm very sad I'm very angry. When we tried to leave the emergency room, it was like trying to escape a maze, and we found we couldn't get out. There were arrows hand-drawn on A4 sheets of paper on the wall, but because we were in such a state we couldn't even see them. We were looking at the emergency-exit signs. The emergency room was very quiet. Apart from us, there was only one other guy in there, alone, and two nurses. One of the nurses said from the station, 'If you can't get out, just follow the signs, won't you!' They both started laughing, in the way you laugh with a friend in retail when a customer can't get shit right. You laugh and look at your colleague and laugh that 'what a fuckwit' laugh. I was really sad, so I was really, really angry.

'Why don't you get off your fucking ass and help us, then?' I snapped.

They stopped laughing immediately and the 'talker' got up, pointed us to the door and said, 'Just push the bottom button.'

When the doors swung open, I looked back. Both were now standing next to each other looking at us as we left. I glared at them and said, 'What a pack of cunts!'

Now I know they probably weren't cunts, but honestly, when you see people obviously distressed and you're in the position of 'caregiver', then it's your job, at the very least, to give a shit! But, in saying that, my response was out of proportion to the rudeness we received, so if anyone is reading this and knows a nurse who worked at Waitakere Hospital who got called a cunt by me back in 2015, please tell her I said sorry, OK? There. That makes me feel better.

Because, when the dust had settled after our horrific night, I felt bad about it — just not quite bad enough to go back and apologise.

We finally got home and I managed to keep my shit together for long enough to thank my friend and get her to leave our house before we both fell apart. Neither of us knew what it meant for the 'pregnancy to run its course', but we soon found out. Julie had contractions for a few hours and then 'gave birth' to a little sac with a tiny baby in it. Even just writing this now rips me up. It feels like I've been poisoned. During the night, there were a few times where I thought Julie was going to die. We didn't know what to do with the little dead baby. Nobody prepares you for it, and sure as shit nobody ever talks about it. I had no idea and neither did Julie — who has a medical background — that that's how it will all play out.

*

The next day back at the hospital, they confirmed that it was all out, there were no traces of a pregnancy any more.

'That's it,' I said to Julie. 'We're done. We'll just have the one child, then, and we'll love her for two and we'll spoil the snot out of her.'

My wife is a practical woman. She does not get swept up in the emotions of stuff: she waits and makes informed decisions. That's the Right Brain, I suppose, while old Left Brain over here is on the floor wailing and looking for a dagger to end it all! Thank fuck we're all different!

By the end of October, we tried again and Ole Fertile Myrtle was back. She took, and, in due course, our family welcomed Number Three. Yes, I said Three, because I don't give a fuck what your views are on abortion or when you think a baby is a baby. You don't tell people you are expecting a foetus; you tell them you are expecting a baby. Most people think a baby is a baby when a child draws its first breath, but to me it's as soon as you can picture that little person in your life, and you make room in your heart and your house for them, and your future plans include them. That's when it becomes a baby: when your heart opens up to them. I saw what came out of my wife when she had the miscarriage, and I know that was a baby. So the way I look at it is Number Two left us and it was a very stressful time. While Number Three was baking I was scared every single time my wife went to the bathroom. Every time she called my name from that side of the house, I panicked. I just wanted my baby.

Number Three (who came along in the middle of 2016) is a little boy, a brother for his sister. Julie and I now have a little pigeon pair, and they are the cutest kids with curly blond hair and blue eyes who play outside with our dog, Molly, a well-groomed golden lab. We look very European, except for me; I still look dark. But they are my family, all mine!

The One About MAKING IT (SO FAR)

Everyone dreams. It was probably around the time I did my first-ever open mic that I, too, started to dream. And what I dreamed of was the Just for Laughs Festival in Montreal, Canada. I had been aware of the festival long before I actually started doing comedy.

So even when I was booked for the Edinburgh Festival and for a series of gigs at the Soho Theatre on London's West End (if this isn't saying 'made it' to you, then you need to re-think your definition of making it), it was like standing on the summit of, say, K2 and gazing across at Everest. But I didn't have to feel that way for long. I had it all planned out — flights to LA, on to Edinburgh, then London, then home — when I got The Call. Would I like to travel to Montreal to perform the Sugar Sammy gala, which would be filmed two nights in a row?

Why, yes, I replied. Yes, I would, although I think it probably came over at their end more like YES! YES! YES! in the manner of Meg Ryan in *When Harry Met Sally*. I was overwhelmed! I moved a few flights, extended our stay in LA (well, the family's stay — I couldn't stay, as I had to fly on to Montreal). At this stage my son wasn't yet one and our daughter had just turned four. My wife, who had never been in the States before, would have her hands full. We landed and checked in to our Airbnb in West Hollywood, I kissed Julie goodbye, packed a new case, went back to the airport and flew out to Canada.

I was in Montreal for four days, and I met some incredible people on both sides of the industry — performers, producers, managers, agents — and the Americans! Oh, gosh, the Americans sure know how to network! I had no clue and I was on my own; Bec, my manager, who would normally have been with me, couldn't make it, both because of the short notice (The Call had come so late) and because she was super pregnant at the time. I did, however, manage to meet Andy from Live Nation's LA branch, as well as Nat, who's a good friend of Bec and had managed Loyiso Gola, another South African act who was on the Sugar Sammy gala. I'm mentioning Nat and Loyiso because they were also on their way to Edinburgh and they would also feature when Netflix came along. YES! I SAID 'NETFLIX'!

I did my galas, and they went well, except that the night before the final gala I couldn't sleep — I had a weird allergic reaction to something and broke out in hives. I had to wait for Montreal to wake up so that I could find a chemist and get hold of some antihistamine or, if that failed to work, an emergency room. And there you were thinking I was just a yummy mummy. Well, sorry to break it to you, but I come bundled with a suite of allergies that mean I need two or more antihistamine pills each morning just to get through the day. At least I outgrew my childhood asthma! And what with all the chaos of settling the family in LA and the fast turnaround and packing a new bag, I had managed to travel without my pills. How sexy is that! But as it turned out, I got hold of the right replacements, the hives left me and I completed the last night of shows.

After a few drinks with Nat, it was time to rush back to the hotel, grab my bags and fly back to LA to collect my family for two more long flights to Edinburgh. That's two nights without sleep, plus long flights, which would have been long even if I didn't have a frazzled wife and two kids under five. If you aren't jealous of my glamorous lifestyle yet, WAIT! THERE'S MORE! I also had really bad tendonitis in both knees; so bad that I could hardly walk and had to ice my legs all day in order to stand on stage for an hour a night.

For these and other reasons, mostly having to do with the pressure to perform and the general high-adrenaline atmosphere of the festival, Edinburgh was both extremely challenging and highly rewarding. It was like being beaten repeatedly, but all the while being aware of the benefits of being beaten — a confusing time for an adult human! It was lucky I saw so many comics I knew, and that our little community keeps an eye out for its own. I was one of a very fortunate few who got to experience the Edinburgh festival with close friends, most notably Nazeem Hussain and Jason Byrne. Naz and I would hand out flyers together. I'd tell people on the street that Naz and I were identical twins who had been separated at birth but who had since found our birth mother, and that our shows were about that and how happy we are now . . . I'm more than 10 years older than Naz. I'm a white South African woman with a broad Afrikaans accent, and he's a brown man whose family is from Sri Lanka and who is Aussie as. Plus, as far as I know it's biologically impossible for a man and a woman to be identical twins because of the dangly bits . . . We must have handed out hundreds of flyers and given this speech almost as many times, but not once were we challenged on it. Not one person flinched or even chuckled. Everyone just nodded and made affirmative noises . . . which proves again that people are generally fucking strange!

> **"I'D TELL PEOPLE ON THE STREET THAT NAZ AND I WERE IDENTICAL TWINS WHO HAD BEEN SEPARATED AT BIRTH."**

Despite the good company I kept, Nat had to talk me down a few times, what with gigging every night and juggling family by day. Julie's family are from the area, so we did family things — visiting uncles and hanging with in-laws. My son turned one while we were there, my daughter got her first wiggly tooth and Julie and I discovered tea cakes. It was a full-on time! It was a good experience, but a hard one. I sold out most of my run and actually made money, which is almost completely unheard of at Edinburgh.

Then, at the end of the whole mad month, it was time to load up the family and head off to London for the week so I could perform at the Soho. To be honest, I hadn't even given London a thought, so all-consuming was Edinburgh. But by the time I arrived, the audience numbers had been growing. I ran into Nat one day in the street in Soho. (In New Zealand, that shit happens all the time: 'Oh, honey. I ran into Teresa today.' And you'll hear back, 'Oh, yeah, I saw her mom

Nazeem Hussain and I have performed in a few countries together. This is us in Montreal, Canada, where we filmed our Netflix specials.

yesterday.' But in London that shit is unheard of!) Nat, like most women in the industry, was an absolute lifesaver. I was so lucky to have someone who could keep her head in the game while I slowly (at pace) lost my mind; she rang the box office every day to get my numbers.

In fact, while I'm saying my thank yous, I should mention the others who keep it all running smoothly against the odds. There's my publicist, Hannah Watkins, who makes me playlists and talks to me and sends me video clips of herself jamming out to eighties music, and who sends her brother Josh round to my house in Auckland for a feed, and whose mother sent me feedback (all positive) about the first edition of my book. I know I can count on the whole Watkins family to be in my corner if and when required. Even if they do all have diva tendencies, I'll take them anyway! I'm also lucky to have Katie Minchin in the team; she will let me crash in her spare room and make me cup after cup of tea and chat to me till we have nothing left. Her entire family come to my shows. Once, when I went for a personal best in saying 'CUNT' as many times in a show as humanly possible and it had been my dirtiest show ever and I'd done an encore (OK, I just put that in there, all nonchalant — to say nothing of using the word 'nonchalant' — thinking 'they won't notice this humble brag') I found out that Katie's whole family, from brothers and sisters-in-law to parents, were there for her dad's seventieth birthday. They remain supportive and loving anyway! So, too, do the rest of the Live Nation women — Mel Velissaris, who might struggle to work an air-conditioning pad with only 'on' and 'off' for options, somehow keeps my social media ticking along while I'm eyeball deep in media appointments (by that I mean playing golf on festival mornings). Marnie — I'm not even sure what Marnie does, but she's there and she's tiny and she makes sure of things. Tom, Charney and all the women (and some of the dudes) at Live Nation have worked hard to make sure I stay at the top of my game and my shows keep growing.

Anyway. After London, the family and I had a three-week holiday in South Africa and Disneyland, and when we finally got home we were so tired that our poor dog hardly knew us (well, she knew us. She just struggled to move, because my mom is a feeder — I KNOW, RIGHT — and she gained about eight kilos, which is a lot for any dog, let alone a two-year-old golden Labrador). I'd had four months of intense comedy life and I thought that I had reached the top of the mountain. The year 2017 had been bigger than I could have imagined possible, and certainly far bigger than I thought I deserved after nine years of comedy. I was tired and happy and hoping that the next year would not disappoint.

Well, 2018 — the year I celebrated ten years in comedy — hit me like a truck running downhill with no brakes and a full payload after someone spilled oil on the road. You get it: it smashed the fuck out of any expectations I could have had, ever!

It found me one morning in my yard while I was in my dungarees (got my lesbian card in 2002 but don't often wear the uniform), using a hired hydraulic log splitter to split three cubic metres of firewood. I felt the phone vibrate, and I had to rip off a number of items of safety gear — gloves, visor, helmet, earmuffs — just to answer it. It was THE CALL (all caps, not just initials). Would I possibly be interested in doing a thirty-minute Netflix special as part of an International Comedy series called Comedians of the World, to be launched worldwide on New Year's Day, 2019 . . .?

I have never been so excited and petrified over a gig in my life. I immediately started panicking! What could I possibly do? What could I say?

I started watching other specials, which only made me more scared. I needed to sort my outfit, so I phoned my straight wife, Irene Pink. Once she'd sussed what I would wear, I found I could sit down and write down all my 'best of' material. As any performer will understand, the minute you put together a best-of compilation for any screen or show, you immediately start questioning why the fuck you chose any of it! But I was OK with my choices in the end.

I flew to Montreal. Bec was there, along with Katie and my brother from another mother, Nazeem. Loyiso was there too, and so was Nat, so it was like a mini reunion! Katie, Bec, Naz and I hung out most of the time. We attended a lot of industry parties together and schmoozed (I'm terrible at this activity: I'm way too honest, and my boredom shows). Bec and I enjoyed the salmon salad — the comedy gods should have made it a mousse — and, of course, we got food poisoning. We nearly died overnight. Well, OK, we didn't nearly die, but I did vomit a lot in the shower, which made me nearly die from being so fucking grossed out! The worst part was that I had to do a photoshoot for the promo of my special the next morning. I was still sick. I was sweating profusely and my hair and make-up wouldn't set because of the cold sweat and high temperature I was rocking. It was only partly the sickness. The rest was the stress that anyone might feel if you had a roomful of Netflix execs looking you over. I kept expecting them to say, 'You cannot do this shoot' and imagining a keen young comic waiting in the wings for the moment where my special would be pulled so he could step forward and say, 'I can do it!' Then I'd have to challenge him to a fight in my shower, which was then knee-deep in . . . for once, I'll spare you the disgusting details. But the execs simply said, 'You look like you need meds and a rest.'

The venue in Montreal where our Netflix specials were filmed.

Team Canada: Nazeem Hussain, Bec Sutherland, Katie Minchin and me.

Interviewing Malcolm Turnbull for SBS TV at Sydney's Mardi Gras in 2018. I was one of four hosts, and the only one working Oxford Street.

Opportunity knocks: at the same event in 2018, I turned and locked eyes with Cher! And I interviewed her and made her laugh! My work here is done . . .

They were right. I got up at four in the morning feeling better, got ready, did the promo shoot, had my make-up and hair done, and then recorded two back-to-back specials with new audiences every time. I was so exhausted that right after my record I fell asleep in the green room next to another comic . . . I had zero fucks to give at this point!

Now you'd think that the minute a special comes out, BOOM! Life changing! Oprah-rich, Kardashian-famous with a boob lift booked in (I don't need it, your mum needs it!) . . . But who knows. I could be one of those who slip under the radar. Very few people may watch it. The fact of the matter is, whether it goes off or not, it's something that no one can take from me: I have a Netflix special to my name and, as a comic, that shit looks amazing on a CV! If anyone ever asks me for a CV, I'll be stoked and ready to roll!

I'm very happy that I got to do it with good friends; we will always have French Canada. I also learned a lot from the whole experience. If nothing else, I got to fly business class all the way from Auckland, so I'm fucked for life. I'll never sit in the back again.

In a perfect world, though, if anyone from Netflix reads this, I would love to record a special in the Melbourne Town Hall. That's my comedy home. The audiences there are my people, and Australians will travel from Cairns to come and see me at the Town Hall. I mean, I love the Opera House in Sydney, but she gets all the cool shit! Give me the ugly sister (aka the Town Hall) any day!

EPILOGUE

You would think, having spent half my life — maybe more — in advertising that I would be a natural-born writer. Like hell! I do write. I try to write a bit every day, and I'm always writing down ideas for gags. I trust myself enough now that I don't feel the need to write down a whole show. Instead, I back myself to work from just a set list.

Anyway. What I'm trying to say is that no one is more surprised than myself to find that I'm at the end of the book. There are two reasons for this. One: I have no idea what I'm doing. And Two: the book never ends. Shit keeps happening that I want to add in. 'Oh,' you might say. 'There'll be other books for all that stuff,' but my answer to you would be, 'Fuck off.' There will only ever be one book, because this one has been a hell of a process and I'm not convinced I'm enjoying it.

Still. I think I owe it to anyone who has got this far to cover off certain loose ends.

Around the time that my son was born, I learned that my father was in hospital back in South Africa, dying of cancer. I heard he was all tearful and prayerful and all about making things right. I never wished this slow, lingering death on him. On the contrary, I wanted the abusive asshole to die quickly so that there would be no time for repentance and he would therefore burn in hell. That way, I wouldn't have to waste my time hating him.

Well, I have news on that front. On 2 May 2016, my father died.

I was driving back from a weekend away with my wife and daughter, and my mother rang and said, 'It's over' and I knew without having to ask what she meant. He was gone. I immediately felt sadness and relief. It was the weirdest experience I'd ever had.

Contrary to what many of you might think, based on your amateur psychological notions of lesbyterianism, I don't have any daddy issues at all. But the same can't be said for Reinette, my sister. When I learned the news, I was on my way to see her, because she too was in hospital, gravely ill. My mother asked me to assess her and see if I thought she was strong enough to handle the news.

Once I got to the hospital, I sat in the foyer for a long time just staring at my shoes and processing what had happened and what I needed to do. I thought, 'What would I want, if I was my sister and the rest of the family knew this big piece of news about someone who, quite frankly, was fifty per cent of the reason I am here today? What would I want?' And I thought, 'I'm just gonna tell her, regardless of her state.' I went up to her room and we chatted for a little bit. She did not look good, she was as sick as anything, and I just said, 'Dad's dead.'

There was a bit of a pause, then she said, 'Well, good. Nobody will mourn him.'

I wish I could leave a couple of pages empty after this statement to show how I felt in that moment. Just empty, complete emptiness.

I said that I thought we should all process it, though. He died alone, nobody gave a shit. My grandmother — his mom — would mourn him, but ultimately most people just felt as Reinette did: 'Well, that's done.' I felt sad, on a theoretical level. I felt sad for the waste of a perfectly good life. Unlike lots of people, he got given a good body and mind and he did nothing with them. That's a crying shame.

So we moved on. That constant fear that he might pop back into our lives was gone forever, but the fact that I was now half an orphan couldn't be ignored. I was sad — still am — and I mourned who he could have been, not who he was.

In the end, he had his punishment. He didn't have the privilege of seeing my siblings and I grow into adults and parents and partners, and he was never part of our lives. He'll never get to meet any of his grandbabies, and he will have died with the knowledge that I taught all of them, as soon as they were ready (from the age of 18 months and up), to say 'Ben is a dipshit.' OK, so I suppose I do have a few issues to work through, but grief for the man who used to beat me with a sjambok (a traditional Afrikaner stock whip) till blood poured down my back is not one of them.

*

Benjamin Christoffel Carlson. (He passed away in May 2016.)

I went back to South Africa in September 2018 to collect my dad's personal belongings. There were some CVs in there and some photos of us as children that, unbeknown to me, some of the aunties had sent him. That was basically it. To be able to fit your entire life into a black file, only for most of it to be trash that can be thrown out, is very sad. What I did realise then is that it truly is only the good who die young.

My cousins and aunties who were at the lunch where I collected my dad's effects were super positive about his life. They were talking about him as though he were the best man ever to walk the face of the earth. He was so talented and loving and helpful . . .

I couldn't cope! I nearly vomited in my own shoes.

'Let's not forget he was an abusive asshole and he did nothing for his children,' I chipped in. But even as I said it, I realised that this was their process. They needed to say positive things about him, if only to try to wipe his shit out of their lives.

My favourite auntie, Tannie Emsie, lives in Roodepoort on the West Rand of Johannesburg, but her husband, Oom Derek, my favourite uncle (there was never much competition, to be fair) recently died from dementia. I support my auntie where I can, both financially and emotionally. She was (and is) such a big part of our family that I can't imagine failing to be there for her the way she was there for so many of our family members — even my father, who she took in when I swear God himself would have slammed the door.

*

Me and Oom Derek, my favourite uncle, at his house having a braai.

My attitudes to South Africa are much the same. Occasionally I miss the great vastness of Africa and the beautiful sunsets. It is truly an amazing country and a beautiful one and the people are friendly and so hospitable that you almost feel like saying, 'Look, I'm fine! LEAVE ME FOR FIVE MINUTES!' as if that would make a difference. They will still feed you and show you around and make sure you have what you need. But then, of course, there is the dark side, the side that wants to take your life for your worldly possessions, the absolute lack of respect for life and the fact that most people are out for themselves and their own survival and are just trying to get ahead in a very confusing country.

I recently read that South Africa is one of the worst places in the world to raise your children, because violent crime in schools is so rife. This really made me sad and (you know how I roll) angry, because there's nothing you can do about it. And yet, I look back at my childhood and yes, we were poor, and yes, I was treated spectacularly badly by some adults who were supposed to care for me, but at the end of the day, when all the experiences have been weighed up, I had a great childhood! I thoroughly enjoyed the freedom I had, running riot in my neighbourhood, playing with the other kids, running up and down barefoot in the dusty streets (because they never bothered to seal them in our part of town) . . . These days, kids don't play outside; nobody is running just because they are 10 and that's what you do when you are 10. Now, if you see somebody run in South Africa, no matter how old they are, it's probably best if you run too! Who knows: maybe someone just lost their life for their phone or a R10 note (the equivalent of roughly a single Kiwi buck).

I hope South Africa recovers from the past atrocities,

but quite frankly, at the moment — and despite the end of apartheid and the freeing of Nelson Mandela — nobody is free. Where once only a bit under half of the population was free, now everyone is a prisoner, locked in their homes, cars and workplaces. It's almost like the entire country needs to join hands and say, 'NO MORE. We won't tolerate being bullied by the few assholes who are armed to the teeth.'

After a recent visit, I decided I will go back to South Africa every year and take my wife and kids, and not just because I accepted the role of Tourism Ambassador in 2018. I'm not blind to the problems faced by South Africa (as you will have gathered from the above) and fuck knows they have a lot to work on (again, as you will have gathered from the above). But I've also realised that there's so much to offer in the country. All that beauty and vastness and friendliness needs to be seen by the world. It's almost like one of those weird scenarios where you behave like shit till someone else turns up and says, 'Hey, guys. What are you up to?' So maybe with me saying to other people all over the world, 'GO VISIT, GO SEE!' the place will improve. Because it is capable of improvement. Not having been there for a decade or more, I could actually see those improvements when I went back: in the people, the cultural diversity of friendships, the warmth, the art. I was reminded of the absolute heart shown to you by the people, which is just phenomenal! I want to be sure that the warmth — and the freedom with which it is offered by the people of South Africa — become a part of my children's souls. There's love and there's joy that can only be found there.

*

Anyway. Whatever emotions I have owned up to in telling my story, I want you to be sure that none of that stuff amounts to regret, for which (I think I've mentioned) there is no greater waste of time. From the moment I first stepped off the aeroplane in New Zealand, it was my home and I was happy to be there, happy to be raising a family in one of the best places in the world to raise a family. I was (am) incredibly grateful to everyone who helped me get established, whether it was my fellow South African immigrants or natural-born Kiwis. And from those first days as an immigrant, I've been grateful to people everywhere — not least in Australia — for opening their hearts (and, in some cases, their homes) to me (I'm looking at you, Kerry Reid), and for their kindness, their support and starting my edge trimmer. I am grateful to all of the audiences who have showed up and laughed at my jokes, and told me face-to-face or Facebook-to-Facebook that I didn't suck too badly. I am the luckiest girl alive with my career, my wife, my daughter and my son. Not everyone gets blessed with a life of love and laughter, and I'm sure my slipper-biffing grandmother would be perplexed that you can get all that when you smoke and drink and say 'fuck' a lot.

Funny how it works out, eh? Fucking eh!